BEFORE YOU SAY

"I don't believe"

D0452116

ROGER CARSWELL

Published by 10Publishing, a division of 10ofthose.com,
Unit C, Tomlinson Road, Leyland, PR25 2DY, England.

Email: info@10ofthose.com Website: www.10ofthose.com

Unless marked, Bible quotations are from:
The Holy Bible, New International Version®, NIV® Copyright
© 1973, 1978, 1984, 2011 by Biblica, Inc.® Used by permission.
All rights reserved worldwide.

Also from the New King James Version®. Copyright © 1982 by
Thomas Nelson, Inc. Used by permission. All rights reserved.

Also from the Holy Bible, Today's New International® Version
TNIV®. Copyright © 2001, 2005 by International Bible Society®.
Used by permission of International Bible Society®. All rights
reserved worldwide.

Also from the Holy Bible. New Living Translation copyright © 1996,
2004, 2007 by Tyndale House Foundation. Used by permission of
Tyndale House Publishers Inc., Carol Stream, Illinois 60188.
All rights reserved.

ISBN 978-1-909611-54-2

Designed by Mike Thorpe /www.design-chapel.com

Printed in Denmark by Nørhaven

Contents

Acknowledgements

I am particularly grateful to Stephen Wright, lifetime friend and barrister, whose research and material has been used in much of my chapter on the resurrection of Jesus. I have leaned heavily on his *Resurrection – Myth or Miracle?* published by Young Life.[1]

I am thankful for those who have read, corrected and improved this manuscript: Janice Bowman of Wigston, Michael Orr of Maryport and Peter and Pim Claridge of Crowborough.

[1] Young Life: www.younglife.org.uk (accessed 2 May 2013).

Introduction

Some years ago I wrote a book giving my answers to the questions that people who are not Christians ask people who are. There are fifty-seven questions in all, ranging from why God allows suffering, to whether God forbids the eating of prawns, to who was Cain's wife? *Grill a Christian* has been published in different editions and has been widely distributed and, I trust, read!

I am conscious, though, that today it is trendy to claim not to be a 'person of faith'. In fact, it has become fashionable for the movers, shakers and celebrities of society to ridicule both the Christian faith and those who profess to trust Christ. As an Australian magazine editor wrote,

> *It is no longer an act of daring intellectual independence to rubbish Christianity as an outmoded fantasy. It is now a commonplace of our cultural conversation and life; a basic assumption of nearly all the gatekeepers and leaders of our culture. Our whole society proceeds on its way as if Christianity is an historical relic...*[1]

This tide of unbelief seems to include most people around us – friends, colleagues, family, the media and the movies. So we wonder whether it is really possible or likely that they are wrong. And while society forbids the scorning of other faiths – quite rightly – because of fear of reprisals, Christians are known to 'turn the other cheek' and are therefore 'fair game'.

We have also been bombarded with aggressive atheism from people who brazenly insist that anyone who disagrees with their beliefs is 'stupid', and that Christians should be mocked and publicly ridiculed with contempt.[2] They say that only those whom they define as 'elite scientists' can discern the nature of reality.

Before You Say I Don't Believe is an earnest plea to consider a little of the evidence for Christian belief, and to take a fresh look at the claims of Jesus and the impact He can make on your life. The Gospel writer John said of his great book: 'these are written that you may believe that Jesus is the Christ, the Son of God, and that believing you may have life in His name.'[3] I have written with the same intention. At least, I would lovingly urge you not to blindly follow today's secularist agenda, but to consider Christ;

I URGE YOU NOT TO BLINDLY FOLLOW TODAY'S SECULARIST AGENDA, BUT TO CONSIDER CHRIST

that you might come to know Him as your Lord and Saviour, who calls us His friends.

Trying to tackle the various aspects of each issue has meant that there is some repetition of information, but I have tried to keep this to a minimum for those who, rather than dipping into individual issues, read from beginning to end. I am conscious that none of the issues are dealt with in the depth that they deserve, but for those who want to pursue any particular topic I would recommend writing to the publisher of this book and asking for websites or books which explore in detail the questions of concern to them.

NOTES

1. Tony Payne in *The Briefing*, November–December 2012.
2. Richard Dawkins at the Rally for Reason in Washington on 27 March 2012.
3. John 20:31, NKJV.

1

Can you agree with Christians that questions about God are of the utmost importance?

The German philosopher Goethe argued that the defining issue throughout history was the divide between the sacred and the secular.

There is a battle for our minds that has been fought since the beginning of time, which appears to be reaching a new climax now.

Since Professor Alister McGrath published his highly acclaimed book *The Twilight of Atheism* in 2004, atheism has risen up again in the West to attack traditional beliefs in God. The mass media have paraded model atheists on our television screens, our radio stations and in our newspapers and magazines. In Britain, the BBC particularly seems to be at the forefront of a continuing, unrelenting attack on Christian beliefs and standards. Also, university lecturers and schoolteachers have felt emboldened in their cynicism towards Christianity. (For example, one university sends an atheistic book to all freshers before arriving for their first year of study.) There is an attempt to airbrush Christianity from society and history.

The result is that generations have grown up who are ignorant of the Bible's message. They are unable to recognise even the simplest Bible story, and know little about the life and work, death and resurrection of Jesus Christ. Curiously, they have within them an antagonism towards Christianity, something about which they actually know very little.

And yet there is an awareness that society is fractured and, despite so much that is good, there are issues which secular humanism has not been able to answer. Without a Creator, it is impossible to have absolute standards of right and wrong, so society falls into line with the situational ethics of current whims. In mid September 2012, two policewomen were murdered while following up a routine call in Manchester. Local clergyman, Revd James Halstead appeared on the television news that night and later wrote:

> WITHOUT A CREATOR, IT IS IMPOSSIBLE TO HAVE ABSOLUTE STANDARDS OF RIGHT AND WRONG

The events which have brought the nation's media to our doorstep in these last weeks have been deeply shocking, not only for the families of Fiona Bone and Nicola Hughes, but also for our community and for the nation as a whole.

Here is tragedy, pain and confusion in heavy measure.

. . . this is not a terrible area. Yes, this is a broken area – but as Christians we believe the whole world is a broken world... we're not perfect in Mottram Parish – but that's where the gospel begins: nobody is. As Christians we have the only possible way of beginning to 'explain' these events (though, even with the wisdom of God on our side, we can barely hope to fully understand). But we begin with a grasp of our brokenness, our fallenness. Though we haven't shot innocent police officers, we all have minds and hearts distorted in some ways. But even as we are present and care for those affected by this tragedy, so too we have a God who cares enough for us that he comes to be present among us, to redeem us, to restore us. My walking onto Ashworth Lane that day was a very small sign, the tiniest reflection of God's walk into this world – born as a baby, to grow and be a man amongst God's people. Then ultimately to die – innocent and in the service of his people – to make us new. Good may come of these events, especially if it draws our communities closer together. But only the good news about Jesus Christ helps us find real and lasting hope in times like these.

In times of grief, fear and uncertainty, it is appropriate to defend a community against shaming accusations, provide comfort and hope to those affected, and to speak of the gracious work of God in the Lord Jesus Christ to redeem and restore a broken and sin-infected world.

Belief in God will hugely impact the behaviour of individuals and society and its laws. Most young people today, for example, are taught about slavery. However, they are not taught that William Wilberforce, while a Member of Parliament, worked for the abolition of slavery *after* he had come to know God, and that his conversion changed him from being a self-seeking politician to a campaigner who started seventy charities to improve the lot of people and animals. Wilberforce, in becoming a Christian, had his eyes opened to the evils in society which he

WILBERFORCE, IN BECOMING A CHRISTIAN, HAD HIS EYES OPENED TO THE EVILS IN SOCIETY

had previously accepted as normal. Then, with the increasing Christian consensus in the land, he was able to bring reform in the country through legislation and his own creative endeavour.

Christian belief, though, is not about social conformity. True religion will never be an opiate to the masses. Where there is a Christian consensus, society will inevitably change. For instance, during the Welsh revival in 1904–05, 100,000 people were converted to Christ within just six months, and magistrates' courts literally found themselves with no crimes to judge, such was the impact on society. A Christian consensus will stir up a desire for righteousness and justice, godliness and compassion which will be an irritant to the status quo. But real Christian faith brings about a transformation in individuals so that they experience forgiveness and a new passion to follow and serve their Lord. Throughout history, people have found this to be their experience, and in the twenty-first century there are countless stories of how people have asked Jesus Christ to become their Lord and Saviour, experiencing Him who has radically turned around their lives and profoundly influenced their journey through earthly living towards eternal life.

When Professor Verna Wright, a medical professor at Leeds University, was asked what the benefits of his Christian belief were, his first response was: 'It gives comfort to a dying man.' Who or what, apart from God, can give meaning to life – and then to death? John Wesley, the eighteenth-century Christian preacher, mused: 'Our people die well!' Genuine Christians have a confidence even in death, knowing that they have been made right with God through the death and resurrection of Jesus.

WHO OR WHAT, APART FROM GOD, CAN GIVE MEANING TO LIFE – AND THEN TO DEATH?

Writer and literary critic A.N. Wilson shared his own journey on spiritual issues in the *Daily Mail* on 11 April 2009 under the title, 'Religion of hatred: Why we should no longer be cowed by the chattering classes ruling Britain who sneer at Christianity'. Here are some extracts from that article:

For much of my life, I, too, have been one of those who did not believe. It was in my young manhood that I began to wonder how much of the Easter story I accepted, and in my 30s I lost any religious belief whatsoever.

Like many people who lost faith, I felt anger with myself for having been 'conned' by such a story. I began to rail against Christianity, and wrote a book, entitled 'Jesus', which endeavoured to establish that he had been no more than a messianic prophet who had well and truly failed, and died.

Why did I, along with so many others, become so dismissive of Christianity?

Like most educated people in Britain and Northern Europe (I was born in 1950), I have grown up in a culture that is overwhelmingly secular and anti-religious. The universities, broadcasters and media generally are not merely non-religious, they are positively anti.

To my shame, I believe it was this that made me lose faith and heart in my youth. It felt so uncool to be religious.

With the mentality of a child in the playground, I felt at some visceral level that being religious was unsexy, like having spots or wearing specs.

This playground attitude accounts for much of the attitude towards Christianity that you pick up, say, from the alternative comedians, and the casual light blasphemy of jokes on TV or radio.

It also lends weight to the fervour of the anti-God fanatics, such as the writer Christopher Hitchens and the geneticist Richard Dawkins, who think all the evil in the world is actually caused by religion.

The vast majority of media pundits and intelligentsia in Britain are unbelievers, many of them quite fervent in their hatred of religion itself.

The Guardian's fanatical feminist-in-chief, Polly Toynbee, is one of the most dismissive of religion and Christianity in particular. She is president of the British Humanist Association, an associate of the National Secular Society and openly scornful of the millions of Britons who will quietly proclaim their faith in church [on Sunday].

Self-satisfied TV personalities like Jo Brand are openly non-believers.

For ten or 15 of my middle years, I, too, was one of the mockers. But, as time passed, I found myself going back to church, although at first only as a fellow traveller with the believers, not as one who shared the faith that Jesus *had truly risen from the grave. Some time over the past five or six years – I could not tell you exactly when – I found that I had changed.*

My own return to faith has surprised no one more than myself. Why did I return to it? Partially, perhaps it is no more than the confidence I have gained with age.

Rather than being cowed by them, I relish the notion that, by asserting a belief in the risen Christ, I am defying all the liberal clever-clogs on the block: cutting-edge novelists such as Martin Amis; foul-mouthed, self-satisfied TV presenters such as Jonathan Ross and Jo Brand; and the smug, tieless architects of so much television output.

But there is more to it than that. My belief has come about in large measure because of the lives and examples of people I have known – not the famous, not saints, but friends and relations who have lived, and faced death, in the light of the Resurrection story, or in the quiet acceptance that they have a future after they die.

The Easter story answers their questions about the spiritual aspects of humanity. It changes people's lives because it helps us understand that we, like Jesus, are born as spiritual beings.

Every inner prompting of conscience, every glimmering sense of beauty, every response we make to music, every experience we have of love – whether of physical love, sexual love, family love or the love of friends – and every experience of bereavement, reminds us of this fact about ourselves.

Sadly, they have all but accepted that only stupid people actually believe in Christianity, and that the few intelligent people left in the churches are there only for the music or believe it all in some symbolic or contorted way which, when examined, turns out not to be belief after all.

As a matter of fact, I am sure the opposite is the case and that materialist atheism is not merely an arid creed, but totally irrational.

Materialist atheism says we are just a collection of chemicals. It has no answer whatsoever to the question of how we should be capable of love or heroism or poetry if we are simply animated pieces of meat.

J. S. Bach believed the story, and set it to music. Most of the greatest writers and thinkers of the past 1,500 years have believed it.

But an even stronger argument is the way that Christian faith transforms individual lives – the lives of the men and women with whom you mingle on a daily basis, the man, woman or child next to you in church tomorrow morning.[1]

NOTES

1. http://www.dailymail.co.uk/news/article-1169145/Religion-hatred-Why-longer-cowed-secular-zealots.html (accessed 28 May 2013).

2

Whether or not you believe in God, what do you think Christians believe about Him?

I remember asking this of an atheist with whom I was having a serious discussion, and as he described 'God' as he thought I saw Him, I eventually exclaimed, 'Well, if that is what God is like, I too am an atheist.' Before walking away from God, it is important to know who God is.

Christians believe that God made humankind in His own image, but that doesn't mean that we can make Him in our image! God is not a Santa Claus figure, or some angelic being with little to occupy Himself. Nor is He distant, disinterested or disengaged from the very world and people whom He has made.

It is basic to Christian belief that God has revealed Himself to us, whom He has created. So what we believe about God is what He has made known to us about Himself. There are many ways in which God has declared Himself, but He has done this primarily through His written word, the Bible, and through His living, loving Word, Jesus.

It is foundational to the Bible that there is only one God. The one God is Triune: He is Father, Son and Holy Spirit. (Incidentally, human beings, whom the Bible says were made in the image of God, are also triune; namely each person comprises spirit, soul and body). Christians speak of God being a Trinity, and in this doctrine alone we find that God is relational and united. We read in the Bible that God is love. If there were not multiple personality in the Godhead, God could not be eternally loving, for there would have been a situation before anything began when God would have had no one to love. In every great work of God described in the Bible, we can see that each Person of the Trinity is at work.

IT IS FOUNDATIONAL TO THE BIBLE THAT THERE IS ONLY ONE GOD

Jesus emphasized that God is Spirit – He cannot be seen or touched. He is eternal, having no beginning or end. He is not subject to anyone, and is Lord of all.

We have further insights into who God is and what He is like throughout the Bible. He is omnipotent – able to do all things; omnipresent – everywhere; omniscient – knowing all things, and immutable – never changing and totally reliable.

The familiar words 'God is love' comprise a quite revolutionary sentence. Millions live their lives in fear that God is vengeful, spiteful, unpredictable and nasty. Yet we learn from the Bible that He is holy, righteous, just and fair, infinitely loving and compassionate to all.

God, who is the One who brought everything into being, upholds all things by His powerful word. He knows the end from the beginning, is never taken by surprise and certainly does not need to call an emergency cabinet meeting in heaven!

Although God has revealed Himself to humanity, there are inevitably many things about Him we cannot fully fathom. He is God, and we are humans. He is our Creator, and we are His creation. He is infinite, and we are finite and fickle. There will always be areas where the Christian is left wondering – simply not understanding – what God's immediate purposes are in what is happening. The Bible says, 'The secret things belong to the Lord our God, but the things revealed belong to us and to our children forever, that we may follow all the words of the law.'[1]

HE IS INFINITE, AND WE ARE FINITE AND FICKLE

God is knowable. Though He lives in His heaven, by His Holy Spirit He will live in the lives of those who call to Him and put their trust in Him. God can be known as our guide and helper. To those who have turned to Him, He promises to be with them through their lives, through death and into eternity. There are no Bible promises that believing Christians will have a wonderful life without problems, but there are countless assurances that God will be with all who trust Him through the joys and tough times of life.

The almighty God came into our world, clothing Himself in humanity, in the person of Jesus. God became a man and made His dwelling with us. He was all that God is and all that true humanity should be as He walked on earth, destined to go to the cross and there carry our sin upon Himself. Jesus then rose again, demonstrating the power of God, expressed in His self-sacrificing love for us.

NOTE

1. Deuteronomy 29:29..

3

Have you carefully considered the reasons why Christians believe in God?

It is basic to Christian belief that the God who is, has revealed Himself to us. Our understanding of God is based on what God has said about Himself. There are many ways in which God has left ample evidence that He is the author of all things.

First, there is the wonder of creation. We live in an amazing world where beauty, symmetry, order and harmony mean that awe and wonder are the natural response to what is around us. Even atheists acknowledge that!

It is estimated that there are between 200–400 billion stars in our galaxy, the Milky Way. The newest estimates, gained by the Hubble space telescope, suggest that there are 500 billion galaxies with about 300 billion stars in each galaxy. The nearest of these galaxies to ours is 25,000 light years away. And did all that come about from nothing? In fact, can anything ever come from nothing? Am I really to believe this just happened? Who is trying to fool who, and why? Everything around screams that there is a God, just as the footprint on Robinson Crusoe's island convinced him that someone else was there.

Are we to believe that the fine-tuning of the universe is without a Designer? There is perfection in the tuning of the electromagnetic coupling of electrons to protons in atoms, and in the ratio of electron to proton mass (1:1836). The sun is the perfect mass, and any difference would lead to our planet being unable to support life. Earth is exactly the right distance from the sun for there to be a stable water cycle. The earth's gravity, axial tilt, rotation period, magnetic field, crust thickness, oxygen/nitrogen, carbon dioxide, water vapour and ozone levels are just right. It takes a greater act of faith to believe that all this came about without a creator than to believe God is the maker of all things. Former atheist Sir Fred Hoyle states, 'Common sense interpretation of the facts is that a super-intelligence has monkeyed with physics, as well as chemistry and biology, and that there are no blind forces in nature.'[1]

To be more specific in focusing on the wonder of creation, am I also to accept that the pelican beak and pouch (which holds more than its stomach can, is capable of being used as a sophisticated touch-sensitive fishing tool, and which has a mean hook called a mandibular nail at the end of its beak, vital in catching or killing prey) just happened by random chance?

Google the word heliconia, a tropical flower from South America, or Sturt's desert pea, a beautiful creeping plant from Australia, or just imagine the beautiful snowdrop, which is so delicate and intricate in design, yet pushes itself through frozen soil with the first promise that winter is over, and then tell me that there is no God who made 'all creatures great and small'.[2]

Or take a moment to think of your eye focusing and refocusing hundreds of times a day with the pupil which is constantly adjusting to the amount of light. Then think about the infinitesimally minute sperm and ovum which met and made you with similar features to your mother and father. Your body began with just one cell, which first divided into two, then four and then kept rapidly doubling. At forty weeks, or nine months, there are close on ten thousand million cells that make up the body, and throughout our lives several billion cells die and are replaced by cellular division. It is a brilliant house in which to live, but just as I do not believe that my own house appeared without a builder, nor do I accept that my body had no maker. Do you?

> I DO NOT BELIEVE THAT MY OWN HOUSE APPEARED WITHOUT A BUILDER

Secondly, we have an inbuilt conscience, a sense

of right and wrong, and awareness of morality. A tiny child is aware of fairness; we know some things are not really just; there is an aptitude, an innate intuition that is, according to Mahatma Gandhi, 'a higher court than courts of justice and that is the court of conscience. It supersedes all other courts'.

THE BIBLE STATES THAT PEOPLE HAVE A LAW WRITTEN ON THEIR HEARTS

The Bible in Romans 2:15 states that people have a law written on their hearts; that is why there is a general consensus with the Ten Commandments, as given in the Bible. People are aware of absolute standards. (If you are looking for an intriguing question to pose to those who say that absolute truth does not exist, ask them if that idea is absolutely true.)

Of course, conscience, that voice within, can be suppressed or twisted and distorted, but nevertheless it is inherent in human beings. From where does it come, and why is it so powerful? Nineteenth-century Danish philosopher Søren Kierkegaad wrote:

> *A man could not have anything upon his conscience if God did not exist, for the relationship between the individual and God, the God-relationship, is the conscience, and that is why it is so terrible to have even the least thing upon one's conscience, because one is immediately conscious of the infinite weight of God.*[3]

The Ten Commandments

And God spoke all these words:

'I am the LORD your God, who brought you out of Egypt, out of the land of slavery.

'You shall have no other gods before me.

'You shall not make for yourself an image in the form of anything in heaven above or on the earth beneath or in the waters below. You shall not bow down to them or worship them; for I, the LORD your God, am a jealous God, punishing the children for the sin of the parents to the third and fourth generation of those who hate me, but showing love to a thousand generations of those who love me and keep my commandments.

'You shall not misuse the name of the LORD your God, for the LORD will not hold anyone guiltless who misuses his name.

'Remember the Sabbath day by keeping it holy. Six days you shall labour and do all your work, but the seventh day is a sabbath to the LORD your God. On it you shall not do any work, neither you, nor your son or daughter, nor your male or female servant, nor your animals, nor any foreigner residing in your towns. For in six days the LORD made the heavens and the earth, the sea, and all that is in them, but he rested on the seventh day. Therefore the LORD blessed the Sabbath day and made it holy.

'Honour your father and your mother, so that you may live long in the land the LORD your God is giving you.

'You shall not murder.

'You shall not commit adultery.

'You shall not steal.

'You shall not give false testimony against your neighbour.

'You shall not covet your neighbour's house. You shall not covet your neighbour's wife, or his male or female servant, his ox or donkey, or anything that belongs to your neighbour.' (Exodus 20:1–17)

Thirdly, God has revealed Himself through Scripture – the Bible. The books which make up the Bible were written over a period of about sixteen hundred years by forty different authors from various cultures. This extraordinary book, the world's bestseller, makes astonishing claims. It says that 'All Scripture is given by inspiration of God, and is profitable...' [4] Time and again throughout the Bible we read that 'God spoke...' or 'God said...' We read that 'no prophecy of Scripture is of any private interpretation, for prophecy never came by the will of man, but holy men of God spoke as they were moved by the Holy Spirit.' [5]

The Bible begins by recording the beginning of life

and the creation of all things. It gives the moral law, the account and consequences of human rebellion against God, and unfolds the drama of God's great act of rescue through the birth, life, death and resurrection of Jesus. It describes how the world will ultimately come to an end, and details the new heaven and earth.

THE BIBLE DESCRIBES HOW THE WORLD WILL ULTIMATELY COME TO AN END

The Bible is uniquely consistent and authentic, so despite the time period over which it was written it has a complete unity in its message. Archaeological discoveries are totally consistent with all that the Bible teaches.

Sir William Ramsey, professor of Classical Archaeology and Art at Oxford University, was extremely sceptical about the accuracy of the New Testament. However, venturing out on many archaeological digs in Asia Minor convinced him of its truth and led to his Christian conversion. He wrote:

> I began with a mind unfavourable toward it... but more recently I found myself brought into contact with the writings of Luke... it was gradually borne upon me that in various details the narrative showed marvellous truth. You may press the words of Luke in a degree beyond any other historians and they stand the keenest scrutiny and the hardest treatment. [6]

We shall see later that repeatedly detailed prophecies

about distant events are fulfilled precisely as written. The Bible has changed countless lives, bringing them peace and purpose where before there was none.

The Bible tells us what God is like: all-powerful, all-knowing, omnipresent, unchanging, holy, just and loving. We read that there is only one true God, who is Triune – Father, Son and Holy Spirit – personal, and relational. He is spirit, and is eternal with no beginning or end. The opening words of the Bible are, 'In the beginning God created...' And in those words alone atheism, humanism, spiritism, rationalism, materialism, deism, polytheism, and pantheism are dispelled. We see at the end of Genesis 1 that humans were made with the unique ability to experience the supernatural and enjoy an eternal connection with God.

HE IS SPIRIT, AND IS ETERNAL WITH NO BEGINNING OR END

Fourthly, God has revealed Himself through the person of Jesus. No other person has had the influence for good that Jesus has had. Millions today follow Him not because they are compelled but because they have trusted Him, finding Him to be as good as His promises, and so they love and obey Him.

His birth – the place and manner of it, His life – the miracles, healings and teachings, His death by crucifixion, His resurrection and continuing influence, were all foretold by the prophets long before His birth.

The Bible makes clear that Jesus is God incarnate – God clothed in humanity. God came to our world and was called, 'Immanuel... God with us' and 'Jesus, for He will save His people from their sins'. [7] This was prophesied by Isaiah 700 years before:

> For unto us a Child is born, unto us a Son is given; and the government will be upon His shoulder. And His name will be called Wonderful, Counsellor, Mighty God, Everlasting Father, Prince of Peace. Of the increase of His government and peace there will be no end...
> (Isaiah 9:6,7, NKJV)

No one else taught as Jesus did. But His words and works were totally consistent, so that He only taught what He Himself had lived. When He told us to love our enemies or turn the other cheek or go the extra mile or pray for those who persecute us, He was telling us to do just what He did throughout His life.

His example has never been equalled. He healed the sick and paralysed, gave sight to the blind, hearing to the deaf, speech to the mute, strength to the lame and wholeness to the leprous. He raised the dead, calmed the storm at sea, fed the hungry, walked on water, cared for the underdog, comforted the grieving and transformed the lives of all who trusted Him.

Though living eighty miles north of the capital city, He

set His face to go to Jerusalem, where He would be crucified and lay down His life, carrying the sin of the world on Himself. He, the eternal one, paid for the sin of the world, so that we might be spared an eternal penalty for our rebellion and wrong. He died as the substitute-Saviour. In paying the punishment for our sin, He has made a way back to the absolutely holy God.

> HE, THE ETERNAL ONE, PAID FOR THE SIN OF THE WORLD, SO THAT WE MIGHT BE SPARED AN ETERNAL PENALTY

He was buried, and three days later rose from the dead. (We examine the evidence for that in Question 20.) He did what no ordinary mortal could ever do. He conquered the great conqueror, death! He who said 'I am the life' defeated death. He had laid down His life for us, and then lay in a tomb, dead and cold, until the first Easter Sunday morning when He rose from the dead and revealed Himself risen to literally hundreds of people (see 1 Corinthians 15:6). God has made Himself known through the person of Jesus. That is why Christians encourage everyone to read the Gospels – Matthew, Mark, Luke or John – to be introduced to Jesus, and God Himself.

Then, God reveals Himself in Christian conversion. When individuals turn from what is wrong in their lives and look to Jesus for forgiveness and new, spiritual life, they find that God has, in fact, turned to them. He becomes real to them, so that there is a living, dynamic relationship with God. He directs and guides people. He gives the desire and the power to live in a way that demonstrates a love for God and for others in the situations that are around us.

Perhaps the most famous conversion of all time was that of Saul (later called Paul) from the city of Tarsus, situated in what is now modern-day Turkey. Born about the same time as Jesus, he was a great intellectual, multilingual and deeply religious. He belonged to the strictest of Jewish religious sects, which was bitterly opposed to those who were putting their trust in Jesus. On a mission to Damascus to round up and silence Christians, he was dramatically confronted by the risen Jesus. His conversion to Christ led to a 180 degree change in his life. For the next thirty years or so, he travelled the then known world proclaiming that Jesus is Lord and Saviour, establishing churches, and giving us many of the books of the New Testament.

Saul's Conversion

Meanwhile, Saul was still breathing out murderous threats against the Lord's disciples. He went to the high priest and asked him for letters to the synagogues in Damascus, so that if he found any there who belonged to the Way, whether men or women, he might take them as prisoners to Jerusalem. As he neared Damascus on his journey, suddenly a light from heaven flashed around him. He fell to the ground and heard a voice say to him, 'Saul, Saul, why do you persecute me?'

'Who are you, Lord?' Saul asked.

'I am Jesus, whom you are persecuting,' he replied. 'Now get up and go into the city, and you will be told what you must do.'

The men travelling with Saul stood there speechless; they heard the sound but did not see anyone. Saul got up from the ground, but when he opened his eyes he could see nothing. So they led him by the hand into Damascus. For three days he was blind, and did not eat or drink anything.

In Damascus there was a disciple named Ananias. The Lord called to him in a vision, 'Ananias!'

'Yes, Lord,' he answered.

The Lord told him, 'Go to the house of Judas on Straight Street and ask for a man from Tarsus named Saul, for he is praying. In a vision he has seen a man named Ananias come and place his hands on him to restore his sight.'

'Lord,' Ananias answered, 'I have heard many reports about this man and all the harm he has done to your saints in Jerusalem. And he has come here with authority from the chief priests to arrest all who call on your name.'

But the Lord said to Ananias, 'Go! This man is my chosen instrument to carry my name before the Gentiles and *their kings and before the people of Israel. I will show him how much he must suffer for my name.'*

Then Ananias went to the house and entered it. Placing his hands on Saul, he said, 'Brother Saul, the Lord – Jesus, who appeared to you on the road as you were coming here – has sent me so that you may see again and be filled with the Holy Spirit.' Immediately, something like scales fell from Saul's eyes, and he could see again. He got up and was baptised, and after taking some food, he regained his strength.

Saul spent several days with the disciples in Damascus. At once he began to preach in the synagogues that Jesus is the Son of God. All those who heard him were astonished and asked, 'Isn't he the man who caused havoc in Jerusalem among those who call on this name? And hasn't he come here to take them as prisoners to the chief priests?' Yet Saul grew more and more powerful and baffled the Jews living in Damascus by proving that Jesus is the Christ.

After many days had gone by, the Jews conspired to kill him, but Saul learned of their plan. Day and night they kept close watch on the city gates in order to kill him. But his followers took him by night and lowered him in a basket through an opening in the wall.

When he came to Jerusalem, he tried to join the disciples, but they were all afraid of him, not believing that he really was a disciple. But Barnabas took him and brought him to the apostles. He told them how Saul on his journey had seen the Lord and that the Lord had spoken to him, and how in Damascus he had preached fearlessly in the name of Jesus. (Acts 9:1–27)

That conversion happened twenty centuries ago, but millions of men and women, young and old have had similar life-changing experiences as they have met with the living God. God, who has revealed Himself generally, reveals Himself individually to those who turn to trust Jesus as Lord and Saviour. More recently, for example, David Hamilton, a former member of the Loyalist paramilitary, found the reality of Christian conversion.

David joined the UVF (Ulster Volunteer Force) as a teenager and in 1978 was jailed for involvement in bombings and bank robberies. As a young teenager he had seen acts of terrorism on television, but didn't really understand why Catholics and Protestants were fighting or why there was rioting. He remembers the day it affected him, for he was coming home from school, walking alongside the river, and four or five guys whom he knew came up to him, and one said that they should beat David up and throw him in the river. Having done that one of them asked David, 'Do you not know why we did that? It's because you're a Prod, and Protestants and Catholics fight each other.'

So David made the decision then that Catholics were bad news. It was a turning point in his life. Some of his closest friends at that time were Roman Catholics. One of them was Bobby Sands, who was the first one to die in the hunger strike, when the IRA used a hunger strike to protest at the way they were treated in prison. If you had asked David when, as youngsters, they would be kicking a ball around on the street together, he would have told you that Bobby was one of his best friends. It would have been inconceivable to him then that they could ever have become enemies. But that is what happened...

David then joined the Rathcoole KAI (Kill All Irishmen) gang because for him, it was safety in numbers. There was rioting going on. Someone had the idea that they burn all the Catholics out of their houses. He made petrol bombs and threw them into the homes of the Catholics. That was his first act of terrorism.

Later, some guys came into a bar and said they were starting a Protestant paramilitary group to fight the IRA, asking who wanted to join? Most of the gang members put their hands up. David did the same. The IRA were fighting and killing, and he thought that if he could fight back, then he would. So he joined the Protestant paramilitary organization called the UDA (Ulster Defence Association), and six months later began weapon training. He was just 17 when they gave him a gun.

HE WAS JUST 17 WHEN THEY GAVE HIM A GUN

Later that year the police came and kicked down his door at night. Handcuffed, they took him to the interrogation centre, where he was questioned. He was to be imprisoned for nine months. At that time, such prisoners had political status (the prison was known as Long Kesh), so David wore a terrorist uniform. Almost unbelievably, in the morning after breakfast, they had bomb-making classes with live explosives, and in the afternoon they did weapon training with real weapons; they had guns in jail! David learnt more in jail about terrorism than he did outside. When he was released, nearly a year later, he went straight back to being involved.

DAVID LEARNT MORE IN JAIL ABOUT TERRORISM THAN HE DID OUTSIDE

At the start, David had been involved with minor things such as stealing cars for other men to use and then burning them afterwards, or transporting weapons across the city. But eventually David was questioned about murder, bank robberies, bombings and hijackings. All of those things he was involved with at some stage. When he was in jail the second time he made the decision to join the Ulster Volunteer Force. At that time they were probably the most feared terrorist group in Northern Ireland. They were very much on the offensive, rather than the defensive, and he wanted to attack the IRA. So he joined that particular group and became heavily involved. He was even using his own home to store weapons.

David was not interested in religion in any shape or form. Being a Protestant meant that he was 'loyal' to Britain and to the Queen, but not to God. Men in jail called themselves Protestant because they were anti-Catholic. To him, religion only identified what side he belonged to. It was nothing to do with God, it was more political. They needed to put a label on it and that's how they used religion. The conflict was more over political issues than religious ones.

David believed in God, but when he visited prison chapel he didn't care much for religion. But sitting in his cell one night David believes that God gave him a revelation of how He had spared his life on a number of occasions: like the time when he was blown up by a bomb that he had planted himself, and another incident when someone else tried to kill him by shooting him three times. Then one night he found and read a Christian leaflet. He went to pick up the prison cell Bible, and tried to read it. But he found the language in the version he read to be archaic. After going back and forth to the Bible he read in the front words from John's Gospel, 'For God so loved the world that he gave his one and only Son, that whoever believes in him shall not perish but have eternal life.'[8]

David reasoned with himself about the text. He thought that God loved the world because He had made it, but it was staggering that God should actually love David Hamilton individually. Overwhelmed by such love, mercy and grace, David decided to become a Christian. The Bible promises to those who truly repent, that they can know their sin is forgiven. He found that assurance of sins forgiven and peace in his life. For a couple of years he struggled with forgiving himself. But David came to understand that sin and guilt are taken from those who believe in Jesus. For the next five years in jail he studied the Bible.

OVERWHELMED BY LOVE, MERCY AND GRACE, DAVID DECIDED TO BECOME A CHRISTIAN

In prison, he had made friends with IRA men who themselves had become real Christians. Upon release, they were going around schools in Northern Ireland talking about reconciliation. People tried to kill them, shoot them; they came to David's home to kill him because he, with the others, was promoting reconciliation. Today David is a church minister. He has known God do miraculous things in his life, such as the way he was released from his involvement with the UVF, when many others were murdered if they wanted to renege on their vows to the organization. David is a completely changed man.

We have looked at five ways in which Christians believe God has made Himself known. It now remains for the honest sceptic to explain the order, beauty and wonder of creation, the universality of human conscience, the Bible's fulfilled promises, the evidence for the resurrection, and the powerful change of life that comes with Christian conversion. But for you, would you be willing to call out to God, ask Him to make Himself known to you, and bring you into a relationship with Himself that is both intimate and eternal?

NOTES

1. Cited in James Gardener's 'Intelligent Universe: AI, ET, and the Emerging Mind of the Cosmos', (New Page books, NJ:2007)

2. 'All Things Bright and Beautiful', Cecil F. Alexander, 1818–95.

3. Cited by Jim Thomas in 'Answering the Big Questions about God', (Harvest House Publishers, Oregon:2005)

4. 2 Timothy 3:16, NKJV.

5. 2 Peter 1:20,22, NKJV.

6. http://www.oocities.org/vcchurch/biblio/evidence.html (accessed 28 May 2013)

7. Matthew 1:21, NKJV.

8. John 3:16.

4

Who do you trust?

Trust is a basis of society. Most actions in life are undergirded by trust, so we are all trusting others most moments of the day. But on the big issues of life, who do you trust? The UK has largely become a Godless nation. One of the many consequences is that trust has been destroyed.

At each election we hope for better things, but politicians have repeatedly shown that they mislead and lie. On basic issues they ignore the wishes of the people. They have fiddled their expenses and, for the last fifty years, have sought to legislate against the Ten Commandments. Do *you* trust politicians?

We value and support the police in their difficult work, but after the Hillsborough disaster of 1989, and the killing of Jean Charles de Menezes by a police marksman, or the arrest and subsequent death of Harry Hammond in Bournemouth, it is difficult to do so. We want to trust the police, but do *you* ?

WE WANT TO TRUST THE POLICE, BUT DO YOU?

We used to trust the bankers, and wish we still could.

I have never robbed a bank, but I can think of some occasions when I feel that they have robbed me! Do *you* trust the bankers?

For decades the BBC has followed what seems to be an aggressively anti-God campaign and depicted Christians as cranks. It esteems atheists, rarely questioning their lives, attitudes and ideas. Instead Christians and Jesus Himself are mocked by sneering comedians and blasphemous artists. But do *you* trust the broadcasters? The BBC says of itself that it is the world's best broadcaster, but some of the dishonesty and airbrushing that appears to have happened regarding the Jimmy Savile scandal may have left many of us sceptical about their self-praise.

Even sections of the church have squandered the trust we had in them. Instead of believing and proclaiming the Bible, some have preached unbelief, while others have been guilty of headline-hitting immorality. Do *you* trust those churches that display a lack of trust in God's word, the Bible?

And we certainly know we have to take our newspapers with a very big pinch of salt. We know we can't trust everything they print. Remember the Leveson Inquiry? Do you trust the NHS, celebrity sportsmen and women, the judges, and each member of the royal family?

And... do you trust yourself? Isn't trusting ourselves a sign that we are ignorant of who we really are? After all, don't we each mess up? If we had the opportunity, wouldn't we do the things that we criticise in others? Look at these startling words spoken by Jesus twenty centuries ago, which explain what is happening in our society today: 'For it is from within, out of a person's heart, that evil thoughts come – sexual immorality, theft, murder, adultery, greed, malice, deceit, lewdness, envy, slander, arrogance and folly.' [1]

There is only One who is truly worthy of our trust. He has never let down anyone who has put their faith in Him. He has never broken a single promise of the hundreds He has made. He is not a disappointment. There is no conceivable situation in which it is not safe to trust in God. The more we depend on God, the more dependable we find that He is.

Corrie Ten Boom and her family had hidden Jews in their watchmaker's shop in Haarlem, Holland, during World War Two. Betrayed, they were imprisoned and Corrie and her sister Betsie were incarcerated in a German concentration camp. Yet she knew God in a personal way. Unforgettably she said, 'Never be afraid to trust an unknown future to a known God.'

'NEVER BE AFRAID TO TRUST AN UNKNOWN FUTURE TO A KNOWN GOD'

Do *you* trust God? It is a question Jesus frequently posed. He asked two blind men who had come to Him for healing, 'Do you believe that I am able to do this?' He questioned a man whom He had healed, 'Do you believe in the Son of Man?' Then He asked His disciples, 'Don't you believe that I am in the Father, and that the Father is in me?' And after saying, 'The one who believes in me will live, even though they die...', Jesus asked, 'Do you believe this?' [2]

Trust and belief is a matter of choice. Today you can put your trust in the God who has given us life and loves us. His love was such that He came into our world to seek and save the lost people of each broken society. Jesus, God in the flesh, paid the price of all dishonesty, corruption and godlessness when He died on the cross. And He rose from the dead, offering forgiveness and a new, spiritual life to all who will trust Him.

He promises to make all things new for those who turn from sin and trust in Him. And if sorrows make us shed tears, trusting in the promises of God helps us wipe them away. Trust God even when the pieces don't seem to fit together. God never turns His back on people who believe, even when they fail and falter.

The Bible says, 'Do not put your trust in princes, in mortal men, who cannot save ... Blessed is he whose help is the God of Jacob, whose hope is in the LORD his God.' It states, 'Trust in the LORD with all your heart and lean not on your own understanding.' [3] It says, 'Trust in the Lord.'

If trust is lacking, would you read one of the Gospels – Matthew, Mark, Luke or John – which are in the Bible? Then rest in God's promises. Ask Him to forgive you on the basis of the fact that Jesus died for you, and ask the risen Jesus to become your Lord and Saviour. Then you will be able to say as King David did 3,000 years ago, 'I have trusted in Your mercy; My heart shall rejoice in Your salvation.' [4]

NOTES

1. Mark 7:21,22.
2. Matthew 9:27,28; John 9:35; John 14:10; John 11:25,26.
3. Psalm 146:3,5; Proverbs 3:5.
4. Psalm 13:5, NKJV.

5

How do you explain sheer human kindness?

You have probably used the phrase that 'no one is perfect', but can you go along with Jesus' comment that 'no one is good – except God alone'? [1] Every individual, outside of Jesus, fails and messes up. We live selfishly. And yet, almost paradoxically, people can be very kind, altruistic, self-denying. Kindness is loving people more than they deserve. It involves forgiving and forgetting.

But where does this kindness originate? If all nature is, as Alfred Lord Tennyson put it, 'red in tooth and claw', [2] and humans are just selfish genes who put themselves first, why are some people so benevolent and kind? We know that acts of kindness can make us feel better about ourselves, but there are many people who just have 'a heart of gold'. Where would we be without care and charity? Isn't kindness a reflection of the character of our good God, who created us in His own image? We are 'fallen', ruined people because of our rebellion against God. We act selfishly and sometimes nastily. Nevertheless, people can be very kind. It comes from our Maker. It is the way we were created. It is a hallmark of God's purpose for us, remaining on us even though we have been battered and spoiled by what we have done and become.

There are other remaining marks of ownership and authenticity such as the desire for truth and justice, the longing for immortality, the sense of right and wrong, the love of life, the compassion we feel towards the suffering in our world.

NOTES

1. Luke 18:19.
2. Alfred Lord Tennyson, 'In Memorium'.

6

Why do you think so many great scientists have been Christians?

Throughout history, people of science have often been Bible believers, whose faith in God has guided their scientific research. I am listing some of the more well-known ones, as recent atheistic writers have suggested that good science, intellectual prowess and Christian faith are incompatible. Whatever your views, I think we can agree that such a view is mischievous at best, and dishonest at worst:

Leonardo da Vinci (1452–1519) is regarded by many as the founder of modern science. Artist, engineer and experimental scientist, da Vinci believed in Jesus and the Bible. His great work of art *The Last Supper* bears witness to his faith in the caring Christ.

Galileo (1564–1642), despite being officially censored by the Roman Catholic Church for his heliocentric teachings, believed the Bible and argued (rightly) that it supported his views.

Johannes Kepler (1571–1630) is considered to be the founder of physical astronomy. Discovering the laws of planetary motion, establishing the discipline of celestial mechanics, Kepler, a devout Christian, said he was merely 'thinking God's thoughts after Him'.

Francis Bacon (1561–1626), Lord Chancellor of England, is usually considered to have formulated the scientific method of study. He wrote, 'There are two books laid before us to study, to prevent our falling into error; first, the volume of the Scriptures, which reveal the will of God; then the volume of the Creatures, which express His power.' [1]

Blaise Pascal (1623–62), mathematician and philosopher, is considered the father of the science of hydrostatics and one of the founders of hydrodynamics. To him is attributed the famous 'Wager of Pascal', arguing that no one could lose who chooses to be a Christian. For when he dies, if it is not true, he has lost nothing, but probably been happier than his non-believing friends. If, however, there is a God and heaven, and a hell, then he has gained heaven and his sceptical friends will have lost everything in hell!

Robert Boyle (1627–91), one of the founders of the Royal Society, is regarded as the father of modern chemistry. He was considered in his time to be the greatest physical scientist of his generation. He greatly loved the Lord, was a diligent student of the Bible and was deeply involved in missionary work.

Isaac Newton (1642–1727) is famous for, among other things, his discovery of the law of universal gravitation, and the laws of motion, and the development of calculus. This great intellectual was a genuine believer in Christ as his Saviour, and in the Bible as God's Word. He wrote on biblical subjects, including prophecy, creation and the worldwide flood.

'WE ACCOUNT THE SCRIPTURES OF GOD TO BE THE MOST SUBLIME PHILOSOPHY'

He said, 'We account the Scriptures of God to be the most sublime philosophy. I find more sure marks of authenticity in the Bible than in any profane history whatsoever.' [2]

William Herschel (1738–1822) was an outstanding astronomer whose work included the recognition of double stars, the discovery of Uranus, and cataloguing the nebulae and galaxies as never done before. Though noted for his kindness, he said, 'The un-devout astronomer must be mad!'

Michael Faraday (1791–1867) is universally acknowledged as one of the greatest physicists of all time. He discovered electromagnetic induction and introduced the concept of magnetic lines of force. He invented the generator. He also made many key contributions to the field of chemistry. He was a deeply spiritual man, saying, 'The Bible, and it alone, with nothing added to it nor taken away from it by man, is the sole and sufficient guide for each individual, at all times and in all circumstances... faith in the divinity and work of Christ is the gift of God'. [3]

Humphrey Davy (1778–1829) was a chemist who was the first to isolate many important chemicals, and also to develop the motion theory of heat. He, of course, invented the famous Davy (safety) lamp. Like his friend Faraday, he was a Bible-believing Christian.

Samuel F.B. Morse (1791–1872) is famous for the invention of the telegraph. The first message sent (in 1844) over the wire was taken from the Bible: 'What hath God wrought'. Four years before he died, Morse wrote, 'The nearer I approach to the end of my pilgrimage, the clearer is the evidence of the divine origin of the Bible, the grandeur and sublimity of God's remedy for fallen men and women are more appreciated, and the future is illuminated with hope and joy.' [4]

'THE FUTURE IS ILLUMINATED WITH HOPE AND JOY'

Sir James Simpson (1811–70) was professor of Obstetric Medicine at Edinburgh University. He is considered to be one of the chief founders of gynaecology, and was the discoverer of chloroform, helping to lay the foundation of modern anaesthesiology. When asked what his greatest discovery was, he replied, 'That though I am a great sinner, I have a great Saviour!'

John Herschel (1792–1871), the son of William, discovered over five hundred new nebulae, and catalogued the stars and nebulae of both the northern and southern hemispheres. He said, 'All human discoveries seem to be made only for the purpose of confirming more and more strongly the truths [that] come from on high and [that are] contained in the sacred writings.' [5]

Louis Pasteur (1822–95) is one of the greatest names in the history of science and medicine, and is still regarded as the greatest biologist of all time. He made the greatest contribution of any one man to the saving of human lives through his discoveries, though because of his opposition to Darwinism he was opposed throughout his lifetime by the biological establishment. He became more deeply religious as he grew older, saying, 'The more I know the more does my faith approach that of the Breton peasant. Could I but know all, I would have the faith of a Breton peasant woman.' [6]

Lord Kelvin (1824–1907) was professor of Natural Philosophy at the University of Glasgow. He established thermodynamics as a formal scientific discipline, formulating the first and second laws in precise terminology. He received numerous honours from the scientific community, but remained a Christian who firmly believed the Bible, arguing that people 'could be free in their thought, in their criticisms, and with freedom of thought they were bound to come to the conclusion that science was not antagonistic to religion, but a help for religion.' [7]

In more recent years, the tradition of scientists who have strong Christian convictions which have led them to a personal relationship with God include Dr Francis Collins, the director of the National Human Genome Research Institute in Maryland. He moved from being an atheist to a Christian while seeking to prove his atheistic position when studying medicine. The fact of moral absolutes, written within the hearts of human beings, that point people to God, led to a struggle that he could no longer resist. It led him to a place where he firmly believed in God.

IT LED HIM TO A PLACE WHERE HE FIRMLY BELIEVED IN GOD

Sir Robert Boyd (1922–2004) can be regarded as the father of space science in the UK. His obituary in *The Daily Telegraph* said: 'Throughout his life he was a man of strong religious faith that was entirely rational and committed; he saw no incompatibility between the honest pursuit of scientific truth and the claims of the Christian gospel.'

Professor Verna Wright (1928–98) was a physician and professor of Rheumatology at Leeds University. *The Guardian* newspaper entitled his obituary, 'For science and Jesus'. He wrote over a thousand scientific papers and twenty-one books, including *Relevance of Christianity in a Scientific Age* and *Personal Peace in a Nuclear Age.*

Professor John Wyatt is professor of Neonatal Paediatrics and a consultant neonatologist at University College, London. He has specialised in issues concerning the mechanisms, consequences and prevention of brain injury in critically ill newborn infants. A convinced Christian, he has consistently argued that 'many modern social malaises stem ultimately from an impoverished, reductionist understanding of what it means to be a human being (created by God), which can ultimately lead to a situation where 'the strong will exploit the weak.' [8]

Professor Michael Clarkson is emeritus professor of Veterinary Science at Liverpool University, and has been the president of the UK Sheep Veterinary Society. He was converted from an atheistic background after reading the Gospel of John as a student at Liverpool University.

Professor Norman Nevin, emeritus professor of Medical Genetics at Queen's University, Belfast, is a consultant clinical geneticist and head of the Northern Ireland Regional Genetics Service. He has researched extensively into congenital abnormalities, particularly spina bifida, and genetic disorders. He is a Christian, an elder of his large church in Belfast, a lover of, and defender of, the Bible, and has a desire that others should come to know God in a personal way.

Professor David Back has been the Professor of Pharmacology at the University of Liverpool since 1994. He established the Research HIV Group in 1988 to study the key areas of pharmacology of anti-HIV drugs and the management of patients with HIV. He was awarded the Lilly Prize in 2007 from the British Pharmacological Society for his outstanding contribution to Clinical Pharmacology. He is committed to making Christ known to those he meets in his community and beyond.

Professor John Lennox is a mathematician and philosopher of science, who is currently Professor of Mathematics at Oxford University, and who says, 'There is a God who is personal, who is good, who is the source of life and meaning, who reaches out to me as a person, and who in fact, far from stopping me from doing science, encourages the development of the mind that He has given me.' [9]

'THERE IS A GOD, WHO IS THE SOURCE OF LIFE AND MEANING'

Science as we know it is a direct consequence of the Judeo-Christian heritage in this world. Even Richard Dawkins said, 'It has to be admitted that of course, science grew out of a religious tradition!' And there is good reason for that. Some years ago, the scientist

Joseph Needham made an epic study of technological developments in China. He was trying to understand how this great nation, noted for its innovation, had fallen behind Europe in the advancement of science. Reluctantly, he concluded that European science had been spurred on by the widespread belief in God.

The idea that science can explain everything is totally false; science is limited, and that is no insult to science. The Nobel Prize winner Peter Medawar said, 'Science cannot deal with the simple questions of a child, "Why am I here?" "What is the meaning of my life?" It cannot deal with culture, with art, with poetry, with history.'[10] Seeing 3.5 billion letters of the genetic alphabet in exactly the right order in the human genome does not lead one to conclude that this is mere chance or accident. There is order, design, complexity, fine-tuning, beauty, predictability, cause and effect in our world and universe. Order does not come out of chaos. Rather there is powerful evidence that there is a supernatural power behind all of this.

Frank Tipler, Professor of Mathematical Physics at Tulane University wrote:

> *When I began my career as a cosmologist some twenty years ago, I was a convinced atheist. I never in my wildest dreams imagined that one day I would be writing a book purporting to show that the central claims of Judeo-Christian theology are in fact true, that these claims are*

straightforward deductions from the laws of physics as we now understand them. I have been forced into these conclusions by the inexorable logic of my own special branch of physics... From the perspective of the latest physical theories, Christianity is not a mere religion, but an experimentally testable science. [11]

Needless to say, he has been maligned by the atheists, but the argument that behind the design is a Designer, and behind things made is a Maker, needs an answer.

NOTES

1. http://www.answersingenesis.org/articles/1998/02/16/sir-francis-bacon (accessed 21 May 2013).

2. http://www.why-the-bible.com/bible.htm (accessed 21 May 2013).

3. http://www.nmsciencefoundation.org/quotes.htm (accessed 21 May 2013).

4. http://www.netplaces.com/bible-history/the-founders-of-modern-science/scientists-of-the-nineteenth-century.htm (accessed 21 May 2013).

5. http://www.answersingenesis.org/articles/cm/v22/n3/herschel (accessed 21 May 2013).

6. creation.com/evolution-religious (accessed 21 May 2013).

7. zapatopi.net/kelvin/papers/science_affirms_creative_power.html (accessed 21 May 2013).

8. http://www.care.org.uk/events/press-release-prof-john-wyatt-being-human-in-a-brave-new-world (accessed 7 August 2013)

9. http://christianevidence.org/science/page/has_science_buried_god (accessed 7 August 2013)

10. http://www.asenseofawe.net/2011/09/27/lennox/ (accessed 7 August 2013)

11. The Journal of Mathematical Physics 18:1568-1573 (1977)

7

Do you really believe that everything that exists came about from nothing?

We have already considered aspects of the wonder of all that there is in our universe when we examined the reasons Christians believe in God. We live in an amazing world. Where did it come from?

Did something come from nothing? Did all the billions of stars come from nothing at all? Or has something (or Someone) always existed? Either matter is eternal with nothing bringing it into existence, or there is a supreme, eternal power beyond our finite comprehension.

It is the axiomatic principle of cause and effect that something cannot come from nothing, that every effect must have an adequate cause. When atheist Professor Steve Jones of UCL was asked on a radio phone-in programme how something came from nothing and how life came from non-life, he simply fell silent until the questioner asked another question. Bertrand

Russell, a noted unbeliever, once said in a radio debate that the universe is 'just there, and that's all'. That does not satisfy the logical mind.

The Second Law of Thermodynamics states that everything in the universe is running down, as from a starting point. Matter is not eternal. The only conclusion one can come to is that there is an eternal, intelligent Mind, which was the First Cause to explain the existence of the universe.

The Bible presents us with God, the divine First Cause, who brought the universe, the world and everything in it into existence. These in turn serve as evidence for His existence. The Bible says, 'For since the creation of the world God's invisible qualities – His eternal power and divine nature – have been clearly seen, being understood from what has been made, so people are without excuse.' [1]

No more reasonable explanation for the beginning of our planet and universe exists than the words of Genesis 1:1: 'In the beginning God created the heavens and the earth'. Who, apart from the God of the Bible, is sufficiently powerful to be the cause of all that we see and know?

NOTE
1. Romans 1:20.

8

Do you rest easy with the thought that without God life is meaningless?

Albert Einstein said, 'The man who regards his own life and that of his fellow creatures as meaningless is not merely unfortunate but almost disqualified for life.' But today meaninglessness is paraded by atheists as normal and almost admirable. The theory of evolution has led many to think that we are here by chance, without cause or purpose, so that it is meaningless that we live and meaningless that we die. There will be a desire to find meaning, but without God it is impossible. Douglas Adams, in his bestseller, *The Hitchhiker's Guide to the Galaxy* came to the rather unhelpful conclusion that the answer to life, the universe and everything was the number forty-two. To quote someone else: 'You cannot be serious!'

For the atheist, death mocks all that we seek to achieve and becomes the ultimate victor over every life. When people rule out any supernatural Creator behind the amazing universe, they are left with the only conclusion that life and everything has no meaning at all. That not only leads to despair but is disastrous, for it is then that one argues, as has the American author, Brent Weeks, that 'when we take a life, we take nothing of value.'[1] Try telling that to the grieving families of those lost at the Columbine massacre, or more recently in the Sandy Hook school in Connecticut.

No, everything about everything screams that there is purpose and meaning, and the alternative view is abhorrent even to some of its proponents. Some have devised the absurd cliché that 'meaning in life is whatever you want it to be'. In other words, life's meaning is to make it meaningful. Stop and muse on that for a moment, and it becomes farcical. Some try to find meaning by leaving a legacy, by taking a cause and following it, by becoming powerful or successful, by serving others, or by just enjoying it.

Vociferous atheist Christopher Hitchens wrote in his memoirs: 'It could be that all existence is a pointless joke, but it is not in fact possible to live one's everyday life as if this were so.'[2] Absolutely right! Deep in our psyche is the knowledge of more; a sense of eternity has been put within us. There is an innate awareness of God, so that a person can only come to the conclusion that there is no God by first suppressing the inward sense of Him and His purposes.

But life does matter, and who we are, as well as all that we do, is significant. Life is short – less than a blink of the eye compared with eternity, or even the history of our world. The Bible likens our life to a tale that is told, or like grass that grows but is soon cut down and withers, or a vapour which has gone with a little puff of wind. In fact, it seems from God's Word, the Bible, that we were not created to have such short lives, but sin against God has brought life expectancy to 'threescore years and ten'. [3] Yet, though we live within the constraints of time, we can come to know the true and living God.

In 1647, clergy from Scotland and England completed the Westminster Shorter Catechism summarizing Christian beliefs. Famously, they wrote that 'Man's chief end is to glorify God, and to enjoy Him forever'.

I have known people wracked with sickness and pain, as well as the most ordinary of people unknown and unfeted by society, who know a joy, peace and purpose in their lives that transcends their circumstances. They can live like that because they have responded to the invitation from God Himself to come to Him and find life. Jesus likened this life to a spring of water bubbling up within them. Jesus said that He had come so that people might have abundant life. With God's eternal, supernatural life within us, the ordinary becomes special. Author Lily Bragge in her memoir, *My Dirty, Shiny Life*, said that after her conversion to Christ, 'the sky looked bluer, and the trees were greener than ever before. It was as though I had been living with muted vision, and suddenly everything had sprung into vibrant, deep versicolour.' [4] Christians have become children of God, part of His plan and purposes, and He gives us a mission, participating in His work.

Three thousand years ago, the Teacher, the writer of the book of Ecclesiastes in the Bible, grappled with this great question about the meaning of life. He struggled with the possibility that life was without purpose, a mystery following a cycle of meaninglessness (see Eccl. 1:2; 2:1–8). But he came to the conclusion that God was the key to the riddle (see 12:1,13). God invites us into His life so that we can be part of His story and plan. He wants, as the Bible puts it, 'to comfort all who mourn, and provide for those who grieve... to bestow on them a crown of beauty instead of ashes, the oil of gladness instead of mourning, and a garment of praise instead of a spirit of despair.' [5]

NOTES

1. *The Way of Shadows; The Night Angel Trilogy* (New York: Orbit 2009).

2. Christopher Hitchens, *Hitch-22: A Memoir* (Atlanta GA: Atlanta Books, 2010).

3. Psalm 190:10, KJV.

4. Lily Bragge, *My Dirty, Shiny Life* (New York: Viking, 2010).

5. Isaiah 61:2,3.

9

Are you bothered that your life seems devoid of motivation?

For me, becoming a Christian at the age of 15 was the most liberating thing that ever happened to me. I came to know God, finding forgiveness and discovering a heart that was passionate for others to discover God in the same way. My motivation was God Himself. I wanted to get to know Him more, to become more like Him, to spend time with Him and His people. He defined me. And for the many years since, He has been my motivation in life.

We are all different personalities, but the 'God of my life' [1] fits the pieces together for each and all who trust Him. If we were made to know God, then however much we seem to experience life materially, socially, emotionally, physically and intellectually, we will not be complete until we are made alive spiritually. It is our sin which has deadened us to the relationship with our Maker which we were created to enjoy. Once sin is forgiven, through repentance and faith in Jesus, the barrier between us and God is removed. We are reconciled to Him. By His Holy Spirit, God comes to live in the Christian. This results in a new dynamism, unction, power and motivation to live life to the full, and creates the desire to honour God in all things. Personalities per se will probably remain the same, but the character changes as God fills them with His presence. That is very motivating!

Atheist and journalist Matthew Parris, the ex-Conservative MP, wrote in the *The Times* (8 January 2009) about faith in Africa. Here are some extracts:

Before Christmas I returned, after 45 years, to the country that as a boy I knew as Nyasaland. Today it's Malawi, and The Times Christmas Appeal includes a small British charity working there. Pump Aid helps rural communities to install a simple pump, letting people keep their village wells sealed and clean. I went to see this work.

Now a confirmed atheist, I've become convinced of the enormous contribution that Christian evangelism makes in Africa: sharply distinct from the work of secular NGOs, government projects and international aid efforts. These alone will not do. Education and training alone will not do. In Africa Christianity changes people's hearts. It brings a spiritual transformation. The rebirth is real. The change is good.

I used to avoid this truth by applauding – as you can – the practical work of mission churches in Africa. It's a pity, I would say, that salvation is part of the package, but Christians black and white, working in Africa, do heal the sick, do teach people to read and write; and only the severest kind of secularist could see a mission hospital or school and say the world would be better without it. I would allow that if faith was needed to motivate missionaries to help, then, fine: but what counted was the help, not the faith.

But this doesn't fit the facts. Faith does more than support the missionary; it is also transferred to his flock. This is the effect that matters so immensely, and which I cannot help observing.

None of us asked to be born. Neither did anyone choose their family, the talents they would have, or even the personalities that would be theirs.

Prince William did not choose his parents, nor did the little one born into squalor in an African shanty town. However, the vast majority of people I meet are glad they are alive. Most of us cling on to life – that's why we try to keep fit, take vitamins and go to doctors.

But we don't want to just exist. We want to love life,

and live life to the full. How do we get that verve? That is the big question we want answering when life seems so 'daily'.

Is passion only for the rich, the round-the-world sailor, millionaire entrepreneur, celebrity or footballer? Actually, the biographies of many of these people seem to mask or betray emptiness. In contrast, the happiest people I have ever met lived in dire poverty in a slum area of southern India. They had no running water, sanitation or electricity. Their possessions were few. Yet in their church, with a canvas roof and no walls, joy, enthusiasm and a sense of belonging to each other was wonderful to see.

Whenever I meet an expert in something, I love to ask them questions. I remember the skills of deep sea fishing shared with me by a fisherman living in the north of Scotland, or hearing of the pressures on a foreign correspondent based in South America. I asked the questions; they filled me in with their answers. So to me, it is significant that when we read the Gospels – Matthew, Mark, Luke and John – in the Bible, we see that time and again Jesus is asked about life, particularly eternal life. Clearly, people near to Him recognised that He knew what life was all about.

Jesus said things like 'I am the way and the truth and the life', 'I have come that [people] may have life, and have it to the full', and 'I am the resurrection and the life'. [2] He even went as far as to repeatedly say that those who believed/trusted in Him would have eternal life. Eternal life is not just life never-ending, but life never-boring. It is life with a capital 'L', where the true and living God, who brought all things into being, comes to live within a human being, giving life its spiritual verve and eternal destiny with God Himself.

Near to where I live there is a famous set of five locks on the Leeds and Liverpool Canal. It is an amazing sight to see a canal boat gradually being lifted 60 feet to a higher level by the power of the water underneath. When a person puts their trust in Jesus Christ, they are 'lifted' to a higher plane by the power of the Holy Spirit. They come to know God, and He gives a new meaning to everything.

WHEN A PERSON PUTS THEIR TRUST IN JESUS CHRIST, THEY ARE 'LIFTED' TO A HIGHER PLANE

Passion for life is possible because of the passion – the death by crucifixion – of Jesus, and then His rising back to life three days later. When Jesus was crucified outside Jerusalem on the first Easter weekend nearly two thousand years ago, He was dying for you and me. Our sin was laid on Him. He died that we might be forgiven and reconciled to God.

Jesus, who is the life, gave up His life so that we might know eternal life with God. Heaven is not a reward. It is a gift for everyone who will turn from all that is wrong and trust in Jesus as Lord and Saviour. There will be ordinary people living near you who themselves have found a passion for life through Jesus. Remember, He said, 'I am the life'. His life can be yours. If you will ask Him to take over your life and bring you to know God, He will.

NOTES

1. He is called this in Psalm 42:8.
2. John 14:6; 10:10; 11:25.

10

Don't you sometimes think that there may be life after death?

It is too easy to become caught up with the needs and activities of daily living, and the agendas of the media and the moment. Vital as they all may be, there are bigger issues. I remember the newspaper headlines on 11 September 2001. They were about the TUC, invisible braces for teenagers' teeth, and the possibility of a politician facing prosecution. They were hardly world-shattering events. The next day the headlines around the world were about War on America. A bigger issue had taken over.

Interestingly, there is in the Gospels an account of when seventy-two of Jesus' followers had been sent on a mission. Covering the countryside they were excited, on returning, about their successful work. Jesus said to the seventy-two that it would be better for them to rejoice that they had places in heaven reserved for them.

There are bigger issues than who is top of the charts or the Premier League. Celebrities, film stars, politicians come and go. The biggest issues are not always the obvious ones. Surely, if there is a God, the most important thing in life is to ensure that we are in a right relationship with Him. If God says, as He does, that sin is serious, then it is vital that our sin is forgiven.

And if Jesus did come from heaven to earth, with the express purpose of going to a cross to die a cruel death, and in so doing was paying the price of all our wrong, then it is crucial to accept this incredible gift and ask Him for forgiveness. If Jesus then rose from the dead, and is alive today, then surely we should ask Him to become our Lord, Saviour and Friend.

The Bible teaches that it is appointed for each person to die, and that after death there is judgement. Jesus Himself will be 'on the bench', and we ourselves as individuals will be 'in the dock'. The issue then will be about what has been our response to Jesus. Jesus purchased the gift of heaven for us, as He died for our sin and rose from the dead. If we are relying on our track record, then our works will lead us to condemnation. If we understood the seriousness of our sin against God, then I think we would begin to grasp why there is a hell – eternal punishment for

IF WE ARE RELYING ON OUR TRACK RECORD, THEN OUR WORKS WILL LEAD US TO CONDEMNATION

74

sin, rebellion and the rejection of God. But if we have trusted Jesus to forgive us and cover us with His purity and righteousness, we will be accepted and welcomed into His Home for ever. He invites all of us to come to Him and find spiritual rest and eternal life. Could there be a bigger issue to settle than this one?

We are constantly challenged to question these basic beliefs. One atheistic philosopher famously said, 'When I die, I rot.' Centuries earlier, the Greek dramatist Euripides (480–406 BC), who was known to be an austere, unsociable character – he used to sit in a cave, looking out to sea – wrote (and note the first word):

If any far off state there be,
  dearer to life than mortality,
The hand of the dark has hold thereof,
  and mist is under, and mist above;
And we who are sick of life and cling
  on earth, to this nameless and shining thing,
For other life is a fountain sealed
  and depths below us are unrevealed,
And we drift on legends forever.

A little more recently, popular singer Peggy Lee sang in her haunting, husky voice, 'Is That All There Is?' She was not only singing about life after death, but she had a sense that something was missing in life itself.

After wrestling with similar doubts, King Solomon

came to the conclusion: 'And the dust will return to the earth as it was, And the spirit will return to God who gave it.' [1]

There are three good reasons for believing in life after death. The first is our reasoning. There is that awareness of something more to humanity than just a conglomeration of chemicals. We refuse to accept that 'the here and now' is all that there is. The lump in the throat, the chill in the spine, the sense of awe and wonder all point towards eternity and God. These are not sufficient evidence in themselves, but they are indicators. One has only to go to a funeral to see the sense and longing that the grave is not the end. So, if anyone does not want to believe in life after death, they find themselves intellectually and emotionally fighting against what is a residual belief to them.

When Alexei Kosygin was premier of the old Soviet Union, his wife died. She was buried in solemn state, with Kosygin as the chief mourner, and the service was televised. Viewers all over the world saw a strange thing happen as the coffin finally disappeared out of sight. Kosygin leaned forward and placed on top of it an evergreen branch – the Russian symbol of everlasting life! Now that was an odd thing for the leader of the world's foremost materialistic, atheistic state to do.

Secondly, there is the resurrection of Jesus. People sometimes say that nobody has ever come back from the dead to tell us. Of course, that is wrong. Jesus lived, died, and rose again. (We examine the evidence for the bodily resurrection of Jesus elsewhere in this book.) Jesus Himself was God in human flesh, the Creator who became like us, His creation, and spoke authoritatively about life after death. He knew because of who He was, and what He experienced. He spoke about heaven, but He loved His creation so much He also warned about hell.

Thirdly, we have the revelation of God in His word, the Bible. God has made it clear that every individual will meet their Maker and be judged. God's verdict will determine our eternal destiny. In the Old Testament we read, 'And many of those who sleep in the dust of the earth shall awake, some to everlasting life, some to shame and everlasting contempt.'[2] Jesus spoke saying, 'And these will go away into everlasting punishment, but the righteous into eternal life.'[3] The apostle Paul wrote, 'our Saviour Jesus Christ... has abolished death and brought life and immortality to light through the gospel'[4] And the apostle John in the last book of the Bible records Jesus' words, 'I am He who lives, and was dead, and behold, I am alive forevermore. Amen. And I have the keys of hades [hell] and of death.'[5]

I love the writings of the Brontë family. Anne Bronte's book, *The Tenant of Wildfell Hall* centres on the life of

Helen, and her inner turmoil with which she, a moral Christian woman, struggled. The problem was that her husband was a drunkard ne'er-do-well, given to cruelty and debauchery. Loyalty won the day, but his dying words to her were that he wished she would come with him to plead for him.

The Christian has the Advocate that he, the husband, wanted in Helen. Jesus, who lived a perfect and pure life, gave Himself for us on the cross. Hanging and dying there He carried our sin, guilt, shame and condemnation on Himself. He died as the Substitute, Sacrifice and Saviour paying what it would take us eternity to pay. Jesus, speaking of Himself, said, 'He who believes in the Son has everlasting life; and he who does not believe the Son shall not see life, but the wrath of God abides on him.' [6] What we do with Jesus matters for eternity.

NOTES

1. Ecclesiastes 12:7, NKJV.
2. Daniel 12:2, NKJV.
3. Matthew 25:46, NKJV.
4. 2 Timothy 1:10, NKJV.
5. Revelation 1:18, NKJV.
6. John 3:36, NKJV.

11

Have you considered Jesus' question, 'What does it profit a person if they gain the whole world but lose their own soul'? [1]

This really is an unanswerable question. And that is the point.

None of us could gain the whole world, and interestingly, when Alexander the Great did, he wept for another world to conquer! Of course though, there is pleasure in attaining and gaining, whether it is land, possessions, pleasure, fame or family. Yet true pleasure appears elusive. Like catching hold of a wet bar of soap, or grasping sand in your hand – the tighter you hold it, the more it slips through your fingers. Alexander the Great is said to have envied the peasant in his cottage, and thought there was more happiness on the plains among the shepherds than in his palace among his silver and gold.

King Solomon, who lived 1,000 years before Christ, gained immense treasures of wealth, power and pleasure, as well as wisdom and fame. As a king, he had 1,000 wives and concubines! There was nothing which Solomon did not try as he ransacked the world to find its joys. Yet in reflecting on it all, he came to the conclusion, 'Vanity of vanities; all is vanity.' [2] So even in terms of time alone, these gains became a disappointment. The actor Peter Sellers said, 'The expectation is greater than the realisation. I tell you straight, when I cry, I cry for yesterday.' [3] We may not have the riches and influence of these people, but most of us take good care of our bodies and minds, which we will have for a lifetime, yet neglect our souls, which we have for all eternity.

So far we have considered life on earth. But what does it profit a person when they come to die, and they have gained the world but lost their soul? The Bible teaches that when a baby is conceived, that little mite is given an eternal existence. However long they have on earth, when the body dies, the real them, their spirit and soul, will live for ever. (Actually the Bible teaches that there will come a day when they will be given new bodies which will join with that everlasting spirit and soul, but that is another subject.) We live our lives, and one day we will die. Then we will be judged, and heaven or hell will depend on whether we have had the sin which would condemn us forgiven. Jesus died that we might be forgiven, so it is crucial to trust Him. But if we don't, what a loss that would be. What a tragedy!

I heard of a sailor who, years ago, was aboard a sinking ship. He rushed to the captain's cabin, broke open the chest which was hidden there, scooped up all the money he could, tied it in a belt around his waist, leapt into the sea, and sank. Knowing that one day we will die and meet our Maker, logically it is foolish to pursue that which we cannot take with us. It would profit us nothing.

> To lose your wealth is much
> To lose your health is more
> To lose your soul is such
> That nothing can restore. [4]

Our souls were made to enjoy a relationship with God. They, like the God who made them, exist for ever, and have intrinsic value. As an indication of how valuable the soul is, consider this: that Jesus suffered on the cross, paying for our sin, so that He could save us from hell. So to lose one's soul is the greatest disaster. It is the loss of an eternity with the loving, kind, generous God whose relationship with us is worth more than all the world. Jesus lovingly warned about hell. (See the powerful text from Luke's Gospel.) He taught that it is truly awful. Political correctness leads most people away from talking about hell, but that does not eliminate its existence. Jesus, the only One who is eternal, wept over the thought of His people rejecting Him and being lost for ever.

There is nothing wrong in enjoying pleasures, earning money and fulfilling ambitions. But if riches and joys increase, don't set your heart on them as if they are yours for ever. Knowing that you are right with God is the most important issue.

The Rich Man and Lazarus

There was a rich man who was dressed in purple and fine linen and lived in luxury every day. At his gate was laid a beggar named Lazarus, covered with sores and longing to eat what fell from the rich man's table. Even the dogs came and licked his sores.

'The time came when the beggar died and the angels carried him to Abraham's side. The rich man also died and was buried. In Hades, where he was in torment, he looked up and saw Abraham far away, with Lazarus by his side. So he called to him, "Father Abraham, have pity on me and send Lazarus to dip the tip of his finger in water and cool my tongue, because I am in agony in this fire."

'But Abraham replied, "Son, remember that in your lifetime you received your good things, while Lazarus

received bad things, but now he is comforted here and you are in agony. And besides all this, between us and you a great chasm has been set in place, so that those who want to go from here to you cannot, nor can anyone cross over from there to us."

'He answered, "Then I beg you, father, send Lazarus to my family, for I have five brothers. Let him warn them, so that they will not also come to this place of torment."

'Abraham replied, "They have Moses and the Prophets; let them listen to them."

'"No, father Abraham," he said, "but if someone from the dead goes to them, they will repent."

'He said to him, "If they do not listen to Moses and the Prophets, they will not be convinced even if someone rises from the dead." (Luke 16:19–31)

NOTES

1. See Matthew 16:26.

2. Ecclesiastes 1:2 (see also 12:8), KJV.

3. The Life and Death of Peter Sellers, Roger Lewis (London: Arrow Books: 1994)

4.http://www.moreillustrations.com/Illustrations/lost%201.html (accessed 26 August 2013)

12

Does your conscience trouble you?

The Talmud (Jewish law) has the words, 'One pang of conscience is worth more than many lashes.' Conscience is that little voice within us that dares to act like a judge to condemn us. It can be silenced, for as someone noted 'Conscience is thoroughly well bred and soon leaves off talking to those who do not wish to hear it' [1] and it can be distorted by continually feeding it with wrong information. But it can be a troubling irritant, like hair in the mouth. It puts its finger on the nerve rebuking our wrong priorities, words and actions. Conscience is universal, and though it is nurtured by our responses, it is innate and natural. The Bible describes it as being from God: 'The spirit of a man is the lamp of the LORD, searching all the inner depths of his heart.' [2] There is, then, an inward awareness of right and wrong, and in a similar way to the Ten Commandments, it makes clear that we fall short and do wrong. Conscience is not the absolute, infallible guide to right and wrong, but it is a help if, because it is either screaming or even whispering at us, we are prevented from doing wrong.

If your conscience is troubling you, if you are conscious of sin, knowing that you are not the person God created you to be, there is a way of forgiveness. It is not through trying to improve ourselves or hoping that our good will outweigh our bad – it won't. It doesn't work like that! Jesus, on the cross on which He died, carried on Himself all our sin and guilt. He paid the penalty for our wrongdoing. Our sins can be blotted out, thrown into the deepest ocean, washed away, cast behind God's back, separated from us as far as the west is from the east, if we simply call on the name of the Lord Jesus to be saved. The Bible says: 'how much more shall the blood of Christ, who through the eternal Spirit offered Himself without spot to God, cleanse your conscience from dead works to serve the living God?' [3] This is what God wants to do for you.

NOTES

1. Samuel Butler, 1613–80.
2. Proverbs 20:27, NKJV.
3. Hebrews 9:14, NKJV.

13

Other than through Jesus, do you have an answer to death?

Woody Allen famously quipped, 'It's not that I'm afraid to die, I just don't want to be there when it happens.' None of us has actually died, if the definition of death is separation of the spirit and soul from the body. But we are all aware of our mortality, and to a greater or lesser extent live in fear of death, and wonder when and what will be the manner of our departure from this world.

Every individual faces two major problems: we are not the people we ought to be, and we are not here on earth for ever. The ultimate statistic is that every one of us will die. Death, like the sword of Damocles, hangs over us suspended by a single thread, and we never know when our time will be up.

For many, their answer is to live and let live with no thoughts of tomorrow. Maybe they hope the vicar will say some sugary, reassuring words at their funeral.

Of course, a vicar or priest is not the judge who determines our eternal destiny. In fact, I believe that many a clergyman at a funeral may, albeit with good intentions, have misled a grieving family in order to give them a moment's false assurance. Of course, nobody wants to hear bad news, especially at a funeral. Everyone wants at least a morsel of comfort. I love the words written in a letter in 1759 by the writer, Lady Mary Wortley Montagu, describing death, 'He left the world he was weary of with the cool indifference with which you quit a dirty inn, to continue your journey to a place where you hope for better accommodation.'

Many people, including religious people, do their best hoping that their good works will outweigh their bad, and that God will treat them favourably. This is the belief of several other faiths, but the Bible makes clear that our good works are not sufficient to save us. Sin and guilt need to be forgiven and cleansed. Jesus' words from the Sermon on the Mount are harrowing: 'Many will say to Me in that day, "Lord, Lord, have we not prophesied in Your name, cast out demons in Your name, and done many wonders in Your name?" And then I will declare to them, "I never knew you; depart from Me, you who practice lawlessness!"' [1]

Can there be a more important issue than settling our eternal destiny? After all, careful preparations are made before making any other journey, but this is for eternity. We are told that there are books to read, films to see and places to visit before we die. We know for certain that one day we will die. We all have a limited amount of time. Therefore how much we can read, see or do is also limited. But this one thing is more vital than anything else. And it needs sorting out before we die, or it will be too late.

Even though death is an enemy, it need not be feared. When a person dies, their soul and body are separated. The body returns to the elements, but the 'real us' returns to God. You and I have an eternal existence. In the moment of death we leave behind all our money, property, friends, loved ones and ambitions. The one thing we take with us is a record of our lives.

THE BODY RETURNS TO THE ELEMENTS, BUT THE 'REAL US' RETURNS TO GOD

After death Jesus will judge every individual. Every member of the royal family will stand before Jesus, the King of kings. He will judge them according to whether they trusted or rejected Him as their Lord and Saviour. Every politician will give account of every word they have said, and all they have done – and so will you and I. There will be no spin on what anyone says, there will only be truth, because God knows all about us.

Every magistrate and judge will be in the dock as God Himself 'sits on the bench' before passing sentence. His verdict is final. There will be no appeal to a higher court, for God is the highest court.

Every entertainer will face the solemn moment of hearing from Almighty God whether they go to heaven or hell. God's sentence is eternal.

Every secret of each individual, from every country and each era of time, whether rich or poor, powerful or abused, young or old, famous or unknown, is known by God.

Therefore *the* one imperative before we die is to make sure that we are ready to meet God. We need to know that eventually we are going to heaven. To know that, all our sins need to be forgiven.

God has told us in the Bible how this can happen.

First, we need to acknowledge to God that we are not the people we were created to be. We should confess to Him that we have sinned by breaking the commandments that tell us to love Him and those around us. We should tell God of our wrong thoughts, words and deeds.

Secondly, we need to believe that Jesus is the Saviour-God who came from heaven to earth to deal with our wrong. Jesus taught and did great things because He is God manifested to the world in a human body. His greatest act was to take on Himself the sin of the world. When Jesus was crucified, He paid the punishment for our rebellion. Our sin was laid on Jesus. He died so that we could be forgiven, and so be set free from the grip of sin. When Jesus rose from the dead, He was defeating the things that ruin us: sin, death and grave.

Thirdly, we need to ask Jesus to bring us to Himself, and by His Holy Spirit come to live within us as our Lord and Saviour. Jesus comes as the forever Friend to all who trust Him, and He will keep us through life, death, judgement and eternity. The Bible says, 'There is therefore no condemnation for those who are in Christ Jesus'. [2]

You need to do this before you die. And as none of us know when we will die, you need to do this now. A preacher used to say, 'Repent the day before you die!' But when told that no one knows when they will die, he replied, 'Then repent today!'

NOTES

1. Matthew 7:22,23, NKJV.
2. Romans 8:1, NKJV.

14

If you were asked to summarise the main theme of the Bible, how would you answer?

When Queen Elizabeth II was crowned in Westminster Abbey in 1953, a copy of the Bible was ceremonially presented to her with the words, 'we present you with this Book, the most valuable thing that this world affords. Here is Wisdom; This is the royal Law; these are the lively Oracles of God.'

The Bible, the world's bestselling and most-read book, has changed nations and millions of individuals.

The Bible contains sixty-six books written by about forty authors over a period of about sixteen hundred years. There are two main parts: the Old Testament [1] containing thirty-nine books, each looking forward to Jesus' coming, and the New Testament, containing twenty-seven books which tell us of Christ and the impact He has and does and will make to people, nations and history. The Old Testament was written mostly in Hebrew, with a few short passages in Aramaic. About a hundred years before the Christian era the entire Old Testament was translated into Greek. The New Testament was written in Greek. There are hundreds of ancient manuscripts containing parts of our Scripture and substantiating the accuracy of the Bible as we have it today.

So, our English Bibles are translations from the original languages which are found in the ancient manuscripts containing parts of our Scripture. It means that translation can be done very accurately.

The Bible was first translated into English by John Wycliffe in the fourteenth century. Later, William Tyndale, a linguist of immense skill, translated and printed the Bible, making it accessible throughout the land. He was strangled and burned at the stake, but the influence of Scripture was unstoppable. In 1611, the King James Bible was published, and has had several modernizations from seventeenth-century language. Today, to make the Bible accessible, there are both translations and paraphrases available in twenty-first century English.

Though containing sixty-six books, the Bible is one book, one history, one story. All the Bible is about God. The Old Testament begins with God, and the New Testament with Jesus, who is God incarnate. The Bible is God's written revelation to humanity. Jesus is God's living revelation, come to save lost humanity. The Old Testament is the account of one nation, Israel; the New Testament is an account of one Man, Jesus. The nation was founded and nurtured by God in order to bring Jesus to the world. So the whole of the Bible is built around the story of Jesus and His promise of eternal life for those who will repent and believe, trusting Him as Lord and Saviour.

I encourage you to read the Bible, or at least some of it, for yourself, and allow God to speak to you through His word. Read Genesis, and the Gospels, Matthew, Mark, Luke and John. See the devotion in the Psalms, the wisdom of the Proverbs. Discover the great Christian doctrine of justification by faith in Romans. See how God describes the future in the final book of Revelation. Read some of the Bible's great history in Joshua, Judges, Ruth and 1 and 2 Samuel. Then let the prophets speak to you afresh. Let God speak to you and thrill you with Himself through the Bible.

NOTE

1. 'Testament' means covenant or agreement.

15

Can you explain how the Bible's prophecies could be so accurately fulfilled?

If I am asked why I believe the Bible, I would point the questioner to the fulfilled prophecies in it. As a student, I remember debating with a member of the Humanist Association about the Bible, and it was the issue of Bible prophecies that I wanted to keep as the focus, with the question: How did they explain how hundreds of Bible prophecies concerning nations, cities, leaders, individuals, and particularly Jesus, have been so accurately fulfilled and in such detail? Bible prophecies are not vague in a Nostradamus or horoscope kind of way, but very specific and detailed, so that statistically the probability for them all being fulfilled is beyond reasonable possibility. Let the atheists and sceptics explain how someone could write in the present what would happen in the future and so consistently get things right, if there is no God who is bigger than time, and for whom the past, present and future are as one.

There are many examples of fulfilled Bible prophecies which I could use by way of example, [1] but here are two which come with the question: How were these prophecies so accurate if there is not an all-knowing God?

First, both in Isaiah 13:19–21, written about 712BC, and in Jeremiah 51:24–26,41–43, written about 600BC, prophecies state that in judgement against the wickedness of Babylon:

• Babylon will be destroyed;

• It shall never be reinhabited;

• Arab people will not pitch their tents there;

• There shall be no sheepfolds there;

• Wild animals shall occupy the ruins;

• The stones will not be taken away to use in other buildings;

• People will not pass by the ruins.

Babylon was conquered in 583BC, having been maybe the greatest city of those times. Its walls were 30 metres thick and 100 metres high, with towers rising much higher. The length of the walls was about fourteen miles on each side of the city. A river flowed through it, guaranteeing its water supply. There was enough land within its walls to supply it with food. It had no fear of siege. And yet, exactly as prophesied, the city has never been rebuilt; the stones imported to Babylon at great cost remain unmoved, though rocks from a little further have been taken; Arabs will pitch in most places but not here, and the city is inhabited by animals including jackals, but there are no sheepfolds.

Secondly, think of the prophecies concerning Christ. Long before Jesus' birth we are given details of His birth, life, death, resurrection and influence. Here is just a sample of what we are told centuries before His birth:

- He would be born of a virgin (Isaiah 7:14);
- He would be born in Bethlehem (Micah 5:2);
- A messenger would prepare the way for His coming (Isaiah 40:3; Malachi 3:1);
- Children would be killed at His birth (Jeremiah 31:15);
- He would come out of Egypt (Numbers 24:8);
- He would perform miracles (Isaiah 35:5,6a);
- He would be sold for thirty pieces of silver (Zechariah 11:12);
- He would be forsaken by His disciples (Zechariah 13:7);
- He would be accused by false witnesses (Psalms 35:11);
- He would be silent before His accusers (Isaiah 53:7);

- He would be smitten and spat upon
  (Isaiah 50:6; Mic. 5:1);

- His hands and feet would be pierced
  (Psalms 22:16; Zech. 12:10);

- He would be crucified between thieves
  (Isaiah 53:12);

- He would be rejected by His own people
  (Isaiah 53:3);

- He would be hated without a cause (Psalms 69:4);

- His garments would be gambled for
  (Psalms 22:18);

- Not a bone of His body would be broken
  (Psalms 34:20);

- His side would be pierced (Zechariah 12:10);

- He would die a criminal's death but be buried in a
  rich man's tomb (Isaiah 53:9);

- He would rise from the dead (Psalms 16:10).

All these were fulfilled in the one life of Jesus. How does the atheist explain these prophecies, made hundreds of years before Jesus' birth, if the Bible is not the word of God?

NOTE

1. See my book *Why Believe?* (Carlisle: Authentic, 1990) for more examples.

16

In view of all the fulfilled prophecies, have you considered what the Bible says about how the world will end?[1]

A newspaper cartoon depicted a horse race. The riders on the horses were skeleton-like, each carrying a sword and scythe. The horses were labelled 'Floods', 'War' and 'Famine'. The caption read, 'Photo finish'.

The well-respected science writer Isaac Asimov wrote the bestseller, *A Choice of Catastrophes* in which he says that he expects humanity to destroy itself sooner or later, but thinks it will probably be sooner.

Unless we are blinkered to what is going on in our world, we know that the whole of creation is groaning from conflict, sin and disease. There is suffering and pain, like in the pains of childbirth. Newspaper headlines can be quite depressing; there are too many people suffering, and our hearts go out to millions who live in dire poverty. Then there are issues of global warming and diminishing resources. We wonder what is going on; we ask ourselves if our world can continue like this, whether God is interested, or has lost control. At times there is a shiver down our spines.

My thoughts and ideas are of no greater value than anyone else's; I have no special insights into what will happen in the future, or how the world will end. This book is not about what I think, but it examines what the Bible, God's message to all humanity, has to say on the subject – and it says a lot!

Repeatedly the Bible, which contains much prophecy (as well as history, poetry, letters, biography and law), describes what will happen in the build up to and climax of the world coming to an end. You don't have to turn to the end of the Bible to see how everything will finish. Throughout the Bible, as well as in its last book (the book of Revelation) we are told the graphic story. Bible prophecies are not to be sneered at. They are neither vague guesses nor the deliberately optimistic guesses of fortune-tellers (have you ever wondered why they don't win the lottery?). Rather, there are very specific announcements about what will happen. God is outside of time, seeing the past, the present and the future. It is He who has spoken to reveal details of what will happen. They are there in black and white for us to read.

Jesus' coming to earth at Bethlehem and His life, death and resurrection were all prophesied in detail centuries before His birth. The prophets told how He would be born, where He would be born, how He would be taken to Egypt, yet grow up in Nazareth. They described His life, teaching, influence and miraculous powers. And long before crucifixion was even introduced to the world, they describe in detail His death and resurrection. They explained that He would die to pay the price of our sin, to provide forgiveness for all who will trust Him. They prophesied that Jesus would rise from the dead, and that eventually there will come a day when Jesus will return to this earth as Lord and King.

THE PROPHETS TOLD HOW HE WOULD BE BORN, WHERE HE WOULD BE BORN

The prophets, as well as Jesus Himself, told us what will happen in the lead-up to His Second Coming. They describe how Jesus will bring to an end the affairs of this world, and then how He will rule over the earth. Bible-believing Christians agree on the basic beliefs about Jesus' Second Coming, though there are intriguing and fascinating differences about some of the details of interpretation concerning the events surrounding that great event. However, every real Christian looks forward to the return of Jesus. Chapter 24 of Matthew's Gospel is a record of what Jesus taught about the end of the world.

In *The Gathering Storm*, the first volume of his memoirs

on World War II, Sir Winston Churchill recalled how people laughed in the 1930s when he warned them of the coming war. The Bible teaches that people will mock the idea of Jesus returning, but at the right time He will come back to this world, not as a baby in a manger but as the Lord, the King, the Ruler over all.

This biblical truth is found in many Christian hymns, as well in the Creeds. When Queen Elizabeth II was crowned by the Archbishop of Canterbury, he laid the crown on her head with the sure pronouncement, 'I give thee, O sovereign lady, this crown to wear until He who reserves the right to wear it shall return.'

The belief in the return of Jesus has given and still gives great encouragement to Christian people. Nobody knows the day or the hour of Jesus' Second Coming – and those who have predicted times only make themselves look foolish – but Christians look forward to the time when Christ will return.

What will happen?

The Bible tells how God created a wonderful world where everything was good, but which was ruined by human rebellion. It describes a deteriorating situation in human behaviour and also natural occurrences on planet Earth. Despite all that is going on, the Bible says that many will feel that their lives are peaceable and acceptable.

Events in the world will build up until a moment when the Lord Jesus will come down from heaven with a commanding shout, with the voice of an archangel, and with the trumpet call of God. He will come to earth with His mighty angels, in flaming fire, bringing judgement on those who don't know God and on those who refuse to obey the good news of the Lord Jesus. They will be punished with eternal destruction, for ever separated from the Lord God and His power. Christians of the past who have died will rise from their graves and together with Christians who are still living at that time will be caught up in the clouds to meet the Lord in the air. They will descend to reign with Jesus here on earth for 1,000 years in what we call the Millennium. This, though, is one of those areas where there is debate, as some Christians believe this 1,000-year reign is not literal but figurative. [1]

In a bloody battle scene in Francis Ford Coppola's film *Apocalypse Now*, a messenger wanders onto the frontline, looks at the chaos and asks, 'Who's in charge here?' No one answers the question. There are people today, looking at the chaos and evil in our world, asking the same question. However, in all that is going on, God is watching and the world is working to His timetable. He has His eye on the clock; He knows the final chapters of world history, and

IN ALL THAT IS GOING ON, GOD IS WATCHING AND THE WORLD IS WORKING TO HIS TIMETABLE nothing ever takes God by surprise.

The Bible describes, in the most cheering words, what society will be like when Jesus rules as Lord and King in His rightful position of honour and esteem.

> The LORD will mediate between nations and will settle international disputes. They will hammer their swords into [ploughs] and their spears into pruning hooks. Nation will no longer fight against nation, nor train for war anymore. [2]
>
> In that day, the wolf and the lamb will live together; the leopard will lie down with the baby goat. The calf and the yearling will be safe with the lion, and a little child will lead them all. The cow will graze near the bear. The cub and the calf will lie down together. The lion will eat hay like a cow. The baby will play safely near the hole of a cobra. Yes, a little child will put its hand in a nest of deadly snakes without harm. Nothing will hurt or destroy in all my holy mountain, for as the waters fill the sea, so the earth will be filled with people who know the LORD. [3]
>
> He will wipe every tear from their eyes, and there will be no more death or sorrow or crying or pain. All these things are gone forever. [4]

During World War Two, Albert Einstein helped bring a German photographer to the United States. They became friends, and the photographer took a number of pictures of Einstein. He had never liked photographs, and especially any picture of himself.

One day he looked into the camera and started talking. He spoke of the despair that his formula e=mc², and his letter to President Roosevelt had made the atomic bomb possible, so that his mathematical revelations had contributed to the death of so many people. He grew silent. His eyes had a look of immense sadness.

At that very moment the cameraman released the shutter. Einstein looked up and the cameraman asked him, 'So you don't believe that there will ever be peace?'

'No,' he answered. 'As long as there will be man, there will be wars.' [5]

Clearly, Albert Einstein understood the complex, fallen nature of human beings. He understood that wars and fighting come from inside us. We are naturally rebellious against all that is right. We shake our fist in God's face, and reap the consequences because we fight with our inward selves and with others around us. The Bible, though, assures us that one day everything will be different. The prophet Isaiah, speaking 700 years before Jesus, told us about Jesus' first coming in Bethlehem, and then His increasing influence, and His return and reign:

The boots of the warrior and the uniforms bloodstained by war will all be burned. They will be fuel for the fire. For a child is born to us, a son is given to us. The government will rest on his shoulders. And he will be called:

Wonderful Counsellor, Mighty God, Everlasting Father, Prince of Peace. His government and its peace will never end. He will rule with fairness and justice from the throne of His ancestor David for all eternity. The passionate commitment of the LORD of Heaven's Armies will make this happen! [6]

John Milton, author of *Paradise Lost* yearned for *Paradise Regained*. That longing will not be disappointed. The world will not end through an earthquake, flood, tsunami, war, or through a terrorist's whim or dictator's pride. This is God's earth, and is under His control, and is ticking over according to His perfect timing.

Throughout the Bible we are given signs to look for which will indicate that the Second Coming of Jesus is drawing near. An expectant mother knows approximately when her baby is due, but the sign that the birth is imminent is when she goes into labour. In a similar way, there will be tremendous trouble in the world in the time preceding the Second Coming of Christ. But when Jesus comes, He will reign with

> WHEN JESUS COMES, HE WILL REIGN WITH RIGHTEOUSNESS AND JUSTICE

righteousness and justice. You will see that many of these signs are very familiar to people who watch world events unfolding. To those not looking for the signs, Jesus will come completely unexpectedly, as a thief in the night, but for Christians there is an awareness of the signs which the Bible clearly spells out.

There will be signs in the world

Jesus said that there would be an increase in wars as nations rise up against nations: 'Nation will go to war against nation, and kingdom against kingdom. There will be great earthquakes, and there will be famines and plagues in many lands, and there will be terrifying things and great miraculous signs from Heaven.' [7] From the first genocide of the twentieth century where 1,500,000 Armenians were massacred in just six months, to the Rwandan genocide in1984 when 800,000 were killed in the course of just 100 days, millions have been butchered at the whim of others. The last century has been called 'A century of violence'. Between eight and nine million people died in World War One. The peace conditions imposed on Germany after that war created the conditions which brought Hitler to power in Germany in 1933 and so led to World War Two.

We recall all too well the 9/11 attack on the Twin Towers and the Pentagon, then the American-led coalition invading Afghanistan and Iraq in the 'War on Terror'.

The late Soviet president and Communist Party chief, Leonid Brezhnev, once said, 'Only he who has decided to commit suicide can start a nuclear war.' Today, we know there are thousands of people who have made the suicide decision for themselves, even convincing themselves that their god will be pleased with them as they take the lives of others. So the prospect of a nuclear war is not altogether alien.

Wars result in a colossal theft of life, as well as a squandering of resources and energy. They bring untold suffering, disease, poverty and misery to millions. They are a sign that the Second Coming of Christ is approaching. One day Jesus will put an end to all wars.

Jesus said there would be an increasing number of famines, earthquakes and pestilences. These are His words: 'There will be great earthquakes, and there will be famines and plagues in many lands, and there will be terrifying things and great miraculous signs from heaven.' [8]

Then the Bible says there will be 'a great earthquake – the worst since people were placed on the earth,' as well as other pestilences. [9] We were all shocked by the tsunami on Boxing Day 2004, yet many nations daily live in dread of earthquakes and tsunamis. As the time draws closer to when Jesus will return, we will find troubles and traumas will increase.

There will be signs in the people

Jesus, in speaking about the signs that indicate the time of His Second Coming is drawing near, said there will be an increasing number of deceivers and false prophets. 'Jesus told them, "Don't let anyone mislead you, for many will come in my name, claiming, 'I am the Messiah.' They will deceive many... For false messiahs and false prophets will rise up and perform great signs and wonders so as to deceive, if possible, even God's chosen ones."' [10]

This is exactly what we have seen in recent years. New religious cults that either add to the Bible or take away from it, but always undermine the centrality and significance of Jesus, have peddled their religions across the world. We are familiar with people knocking on our doors and trying to entice us into their new 'truth'. It is exactly as Jesus said it would be.

The apostle Paul wrote in the Bible:

> You should know this... that in the last days there will be very difficult times. For people will love only themselves and their money. They will be boastful and proud, scoffing at God, disobedient to their parents, and ungrateful. They will consider nothing sacred. They will be unloving and unforgiving; they will slander others and have no self-control. They will be cruel and hate what is good. They will betray their friends, be reckless, be puffed up with pride, and love pleasure rather than God. They will act religious, but they will reject the power that could make them godly. Stay away from people like that! [11]

The Bible speaks of a time of great unrest, with massive

political and religious turmoil. Again, Christians debate whether the one called the antichrist or 'the beast' in the book of Revelation, [12] represents all anti-Christian forces or is an actual political leader who will rule across nations with an iron fist, just prior to the moment when Christ returns to wrap up the troubles of the world. It is dramatic, but terrible:

> Then the beast was allowed to speak great blasphemies against God. And he was given authority to do whatever he wanted for forty-two months. And he spoke terrible words of blasphemy against God, slandering his name and his dwelling – that is, those who dwell in heaven. And the beast was allowed to wage war against God's holy people and to conquer them. And he was given authority to rule over every tribe and people and language and nation. And all the people who belong to this world worshipped the beast. They are the ones whose names were not written in the Book of Life before the world was made – the Book that belongs to the Lamb who was slaughtered. Anyone with ears to hear should listen and understand. Anyone who is destined for prison will be taken to prison. Anyone destined to die by the sword will die by the sword. [13]

There will be signs in the church

Jesus warned His followers that there would be great persecution against true Christians: 'Then you will be arrested, persecuted, and killed. You will be hated all over the world because you are my followers.' [14] Some Christians believe that just as the Bible says that there will be an antichrist figure, there will be someone who will unite religions but will be opposed to Christ and His followers. He is called 'the prostitute' in the book of Revelation. [15] He will persecute the true church. Other Christians again see this as symbolic of all anti-Christian seduction. However, alongside the false religious teachers, there will be the spread of the true gospel to every people and tribe across the world. [16]

There will be signs in the Middle East

There are many Bible prophecies concerning the nation of Israel. It describes its growth, its dispersion, and the re-gathering of the nation and what will happen after.

After the ashes of the Holocaust, it must have seemed that all hope had gone for the Jewish nation and people. But biblical prophecy taught differently. In 1947, the United Nations passed a resolution which was to lead to Israel becoming a great nation again. This was after nearly two thousand years of the Jews being dispersed around the world. Despite hostility between Israel and the nations around it, it has survived and flourished just as the Bible said it would.

Just prior to His crucifixion Jesus prophesied the

destruction of the Temple in Jerusalem and the scattering of the Jewish people to the nations. [17] This happened forty years later, in AD70. He said that Jerusalem would be trampled by non-Jews until the time for them had been fulfilled. The prophet Ezekiel had said that the land of Israel would

THE JEWS WOULD RETURN TO THEIR LAND FROM THE FOUR CORNERS OF THE EARTH

be desolate, but would become fertile again as the Jews returned there. [18] And the prophet Isaiah said that the Jews would return to their land from the four corners of the earth. [19]

Ezekiel prophesied an attack on Israel by an alliance of countries which includes nations which today have made no secret of their desire to destroy the nation of Israel. [20] Jesus spoke about a time of religious desecration and idolatry in Jerusalem. [21]

There will also be signs in the sky

So cataclysmic will be the moment of His return that all people will acknowledge Jesus as Lord. When He died as our substitute, paying for our sins on the cross, darkness covered the face of the world for three hours even though it was midday. When He returns,

there will be strange signs in the sun, moon, and
stars. And here on earth the nations will be in turmoil,
perplexed by the roaring seas and strange tides. People

will be terrified at what they see coming upon the earth,
for the powers in the heavens will be shaken. [22]

One day it will happen. Jesus will return. Those who have never trusted Christ will be lost for ever. Judgement for them will be an awful moment that leads to the verdict and sentence from God Himself: 'Depart from me; I never knew you.' Those who have trusted Jesus as Lord will look to Him and see their dearest Saviour, knowing that they will be with Him for ever.

THOSE WHO HAVE NEVER TRUSTED CHRIST WILL BE LOST FOR EVER

The classical story of the young man Damocles who used flattery to endear himself to Dionysius, the tyrant ruler of ancient Syracuse, illustrates how perilous our security is outside of God. To instruct and warn the ambitious youth, Dionysius invited the flatterer to a banquet and seated him under a sword suspended over his head by a single hair. Those who live but do not enjoy peace with God are so poised before Jesus, the ultimate Judge of everyone.

The big question for each individual is to make sure that they are certain that their sins have been forgiven, and that they are in a right relationship with Christ. Our lives are each characterised by things that are not right: we think, speak and act in a way we shouldn't. We sin against God by not keeping His commandments. We can never be good enough to earn our way to God.

He has taken the initiative and come to rescue us. God became a man and dwelt among us. Jesus came with the purpose not only of teaching and healing, but to die on a cross. As He was crucified, He carried on Himself the sin and condemnation that should rest on us. He died in our place because He loved us. He was buried, and three days later conquered death by rising again.

Today, Jesus commands each one of us to turn from what is wrong in our lives. The Bible calls this repentance. Then, we are to believe and ask Jesus to forgive us and by His Holy Spirit to live in our lives. Jesus is to become our Lord and Saviour. He will help us to follow Him. One day He will take everyone who is trusting in Christ to be with Him for ever.

If a Christian dies before Jesus returns, they will go to be with Christ. Heaven is not a reward, it is a gift. If they are still alive at the time of His coming, no matter what they have endured, they will thrill with joy at seeing the returning Lord Jesus, whom they have followed and served.

NOTES

1. See 1 Thessalonians 4:15 – 5:8, 2 Thessalonians 1:7–9; Revelation 20.
2. Isaiah 2:4, NLT.
3. Isaiah 11:6 – 9, NLT.
4. Revelation 21:4, NLT.

5. Taken from the sermon preached by Dr Billy Graham in Moscow in May 1982, published in Billy Graham, *Approaching Hoofbeats* (NY: Avon Books, 1985).

6. Isaiah 9:5–7, NLT.

7. Luke 21:10,11, NLT.

8. Luke 21:11, NLT.

9. Revelation 16:8,12,18

10. Matthew 24:4,5,24, NLT.

11. 2 Timothy 3:1–5, NLT.

12. Revelation 13.

13. Revelation 13:5–10, NLT.

14. Matthew 24:9, NLT.

15. Revelation 17.

16. Matthew 24:14.

17. Luke 19:41–44; 21:20–24.

18. Ezekiel 36:8.

19. Isaiah 11:11,12; 43:5,6.

20. Ezekiel 38,39.

21. Matthew 24:15.

22. Luke 21:25,26.

17

Why do you think Jesus is so unforgettable?

Not many of us celebrate or even know the birthdays of Nelson Mandela, Neil Armstrong or Winston Churchill, but over two thousand years after the birth of a baby in Bethlehem, millions the world over commemorate this event each Christmas.

Jesus Christ is the most influential man in history, towering over all others. He was born in poverty and obscurity; as a youngster He was taken as a refugee to Egypt; He received no formal education, worked as a labourer, and never wrote a book or song. Jesus preached and ministered for only three years, and never spoke to flatter the authorities, refusing to compromise His message, and was eventually crucified at the age of 33.

In those three years of public work, without travelling far, He made blind people see, mute people speak, and the deaf hear. He healed lepers and lame people, He raised the dead back to life, He fed thousands of hungry people with just a few loaves and fishes; He instantly calmed a rough storm at sea and walked on water, dispelling the fear of terrified fishermen.

Nobody spoke as Jesus did. He had authority. He gave to the world the highest moral standard, preaching only what He practised.

Jesus said, 'Love your enemies, do good to those who hate you, bless those who curse you, pray for those who ill-treat you', and 'turn the other cheek'.

Jesus gave dignity to women, respect to the disabled, significance to children, credibility to the family, and status to each individual. He has made an indelible impact upon our literature, art, music, architecture, and our democratic freedoms.

Judas, the disciple who 'sold' Him, cried, 'I have betrayed innocent blood'. [1] Pilate, who out of fear ordered His crucifixion, said 'I find no fault in him'. [2] In fact, it was impossible to fault Jesus Christ. He was utterly sinless, for He was 'God manifest in the flesh'. The Bible says of Jesus, that God 'became flesh and dwelt among us'. [3]

GOD 'BECAME FLESH AND DWELT AMONG US'

At the age of 33, stripped naked, beaten and humiliated, Jesus died on a cross. As He hung there, God laid on Jesus the sin of us all. The Bible, in John 3:16 says: 'For God so loved the world that He gave His only begotten Son, that whoever believes in Him should not perish but have everlasting life' (NKJV). Christ 'suffered once for sins, the just for the unjust, that He might bring us to God'. [4] He took the penalty in our place, so that we might be forgiven for all our sin.

Three days later, the tomb where Jesus was laid was empty – He had risen from the dead. He was alive. Over an extended period, Jesus showed Himself to many people. He changed their lives, giving peace and hope.

Throughout the Bible, Jesus is the focus. Written over sixteen hundred years by about forty different people, it first looks forward to His coming. Then it describes His birth, life, teaching, work, death and resurrection. Finally, it applies all that Jesus did to our lives and world. The Bible contains four biographies of Jesus: Matthew focuses on Jesus as the anticipated King; Mark looks at Jesus as the suffering servant; Luke describes Jesus as the Saviour who is the Son of Man, and John's Gospel concentrates on Jesus as the Son of God. That is why we do not have an account of the birth of Jesus in Mark's Gospel – nobody was concerned about the birth of a servant, or in John's Gospel – for deity does not have a birth. God, the Word, encases Himself in humanity, as God the Creator became the neighbour of the people whom He had made.

John, the youngest of Jesus' twelve disciples, tells us that he wrote his Gospel with the aim that people would believe in Jesus and, as a consequence, have eternal life. Time and again throughout his biography, we are encouraged to simply believe in Jesus.

Jesus Christ came to earth with a mission. He came not to call righteous people but sinners to Himself. He was more than a great example to us. He was more than a supreme teacher. He accomplished more than the performance of miracles. The Bible states that the Father sent the Son to be the Saviour of the world. [5]

Jesus said: 'I am the way, the truth, and the life. No one comes to the Father, except through Me.' [6]

Millions have followed Jesus because they love Him. Civilizations and nations have been changed as people have come to know God. Most important of all is that He transforms individuals.

Jesus Christ can bring people into an everlasting relationship with God. Instead of the hell we deserve, He can, by forgiving our sin, reserve a place in heaven for us. When an individual turns their back on sin and trusts Christ, He forgives the person, and makes everything new. He becomes a constant Companion and helps in all the decision-making of life. For twenty centuries, Jesus Christ has become the most valued Saviour to people all over the world.

JESUS CHRIST HAS BECOME THE MOST VALUED SAVIOUR TO PEOPLE ALL OVER THE WORLD

In her Christmas Day message to the Commonwealth, 2011, just before the year of her Diamond Jubilee celebrations, Queen Elizabeth said:

For many, this Christmas will not be easy. With our armed forces deployed around the world, thousands of service families face Christmas without their loved ones at home.

The bereaved and the lonely will find it especially hard. And, as we all know, the world is going through difficult times. All this will affect our celebration of this great Christian festival.

Finding hope in adversity is one of the themes of Christmas. Jesus was born into a world full of fear. The angels came to frightened shepherds with hope in their voices: 'Fear not', they urged, 'we bring you tidings of great joy, which shall be to all people. For unto you is born this day in the City of David a Saviour who is Christ the Lord.'

Although we are capable of great acts of kindness, history teaches us that we sometimes need saving from ourselves – from our recklessness or our greed.

God sent into the world a unique person – neither a philosopher nor a general, important though they are, but a Saviour, with the power to forgive.

Forgiveness lies at the heart of the Christian faith. It can heal broken families, it can restore friendships and it can reconcile divided communities. It is in forgiveness that we feel the power of God's love.

In the last verse of this beautiful carol, 'O Little Town of Bethlehem', there's a prayer:

O Holy Child of Bethlehem,

Descend to us we pray.

Cast out our sin

And enter in.

Be born in us today.

It is my prayer that on this Christmas day we might all find room in our lives for the message of the angels and for the love of God through Christ our Lord.

NOTES

1. Matthew 27:4.
2. John 18:38; 19:4; 19:6.
3. John 1:14, NKJV.
4. 1 Peter 3:18, NKJV.
5. 1 John 4:14.
6. John 14:6, NKJV.

18

Have you ever wondered why, unlike other leaders, Jesus' name is used as a swear word?

In the days of black and white television the then leading anchorman and senior statesman of the BBC, Richard Dimbleby, shocked the nation when, thinking his microphones were switched off, he used the name of Jesus blasphemously. The next day it was front page headlines of the national newspapers. Today we would be shocked if such personalities did *not* blaspheme! But strangely this habit uniquely uses Jesus' name: Buddha, Mohammed, Confucius, Moses are not swear words. So why does the Man who lived the purest, kindest, most generous of lives draw the antagonism of so many?

The third of the Ten Commandments says that we are not to take the name of the Lord our God in vain. Listening to some, the word 'god' is very much a part of their everyday vocabulary. I've even heard Richard Dawkins in one of his many BBC interviews say, 'Oh god!' But blasphemy is not 'strong language', as the media would have us believe. Rather it is an act of dishonouring and disobeying God, who has revealed in the Bible that all of us will have to give account for every word spoken here on earth.

As human beings, all of us find that there is an inbuilt antagonism to God and godliness. Like a seed within us from the beginning, it sends out its roots and shoots so that every part of us is permeated with a bias to defy God, our Maker, Judge and Lord. Blasphemy seems a tawdry symptom of a sinful nature, but it does reveal our heart's attitude to God.

The fact that the name of 'Jesus' or 'Christ' is such a commonplace swear word not only demonstrates our true self, but is a pointer to the fact that Jesus is Himself God. Would there be the same contentiousness towards someone who was merely a preacher, teacher or prophet?

Significantly, many people will testify that the moment they actually put their trust in Jesus as Lord and Saviour, their previous bad language immediately stopped. That is the inevitable consequence of God, by His Holy Spirit, coming into the life of the new believer. He gives a new love for Jesus and all that is righteous.

19

Have you considered why Christians make, so much of Jesus' death on the cross?

Stories of self-sacrifice grip the imagination. American writer O. Henry has a short story called 'A Retrieved Reformation'. [1] It tells the tale of safe-breaker Jimmy Valentine who has been recently released from prison. He goes to the town bank to case it up before robbing it. As he walks to the door he catches the eye of the banker's beautiful daughter. They immediately fall in love, and Valentine decides to give up his criminal career. He moves into town, taking up the identity of Ralph Spencer, a shoemaker. Just as he is about to leave to give his specialized tools to an old associate, a lawman who recognises him arrives at the bank. Jimmy and his fiancée and her family are at the bank, inspecting a new safe, when a child accidentally gets locked inside the airtight vault. Despite knowing that it will seal his fate, Valentine opens the safe to rescue the child. However, much to Valentine's surprise, the lawman denies recognising him and lets him go.

It's a gripping tale on a theme which we love, but the death of Jesus is on a far higher level of sacrifice. It was not just a twist of historical fate that led Jesus to crucifixion. This was something that had been anticipated from almost the beginning of time, and had been prophesied throughout the Old Testament, centuries before Jesus' coming to earth. A thousand years before, King David had foretold details of His death; [2] and, 700 years before Jesus' birth, the prophet Isaiah had described it in detail, explaining its significance; [3] others, hundreds of years earlier, gave detailed insights into so many of the peripheral events surrounding the cross. [4]

Jesus Himself had repeatedly spoken about the death that He would 'accomplish' on the cross. These are the words He spoke just after we are told about His encounter with the rich young ruler:

> *They were on their way up to Jerusalem, with Jesus leading the way, and the disciples were astonished, while those who followed were afraid. Again He took the Twelve aside and told them what was going to happen to Him. 'We are going up to Jerusalem,' He said, 'and the Son of Man will be delivered over to the chief priests and the teachers of the law. They will condemn Him to death and*

will hand Him over to the Gentiles, who will mock Him and spit on Him, flog Him and kill Him. Three days later He will rise.' [5]

Jesus was deliberately laying down His life for men and women. He could so easily have called for divine help to rescue Him, and yet in His death He was fulfilling the purpose for His coming. In His death, He was doing something greater than even His feeding the thousands, raising the dead, calming the storm at sea, healing the sick or living His perfect life. Hanging, bleeding, suffering and dying on the cross, Jesus was carrying and paying for the sin of the world. He was *the* sacrifice for our wrong. Sin, which carries an eternal penalty, would condemn us for ever, but Jesus, the eternal One, paid for our sin in those lonely hours on the cross. God the Father took the sin of the world, from the beginning to the end of time, and laid it on His dear Son. In so doing, Jesus was forsaken by his Father and made sin for us, the Righteous dying for us who are unrighteous, so that we might be made righteous through His death and resurrection. The sacrifice of Jesus for our sin was so that we could be forgiven and reconciled to God.

GOD THE FATHER TOOK THE SIN OF THE WORLD, FROM THE BEGINNING TO THE END OF TIME

The cross of Jesus is the bridge whereby we can come into the relationship with God for which we were made. When we think that it was the Lord of all who, for love of us, went through the sufferings of the cross, it is not surprising that Christians make much of 'Christ, and Him crucified', or that the cross is the symbol of Christianity. [6] And whenever there is Christian preaching which is faithful to the Bible, there will be a focus upon the cross of Jesus.

Dublin-born Cecil Frances Alexander (1818–95) was the wife of the Archbishop of Armagh. She wrote many children's hymns, including 'Once in Royal David's City', 'All Things Bright and Beautiful' and 'There is a Green Hill Far Away'. In this one, she simply explains the great truths that Jesus died as the atonement for sin, and that we are justified (declared right with God) by faith in Jesus:

There is a green hill far away
Outside a city wall,
Where the dear Lord was crucified
Who died to save us all.

We may not know, we cannot tell
What pains He had to bear;
But we believe it was for us
He hung and suffered there.

He died that we might be forgiven,
He died to make us good;
That we might go at last to Heav'n,
Saved by His precious blood.

There was no other good enough
To pay the price of sin;
He only could unlock the gate
Of heaven and let us in.

O dearly, dearly has He loved,
And we must love Him, too,
And trust in His redeeming blood,
And try His works to do.

C. Truman Davis, a medical doctor describes crucifixion: [7]

The cross is placed on the ground and the exhausted man is quickly thrown backwards with his shoulders against the wood. The legionnaire feels for the depression at the front of the wrist. He drives a heavy, square wrought-iron nail through the wrist and deep into the wood. Quickly he moves to the other side and repeats the action, being careful not to pull the arms too tightly, but to allow some flex and movement. The cross is then lifted into place.

The left foot is pressed backward against the right foot, and with both feet extended, toes down, a nail is driven through the arch of each, leaving the knees flexed. The victim is now crucified. As he slowly sags down with more weight on the nails in the wrists, excruciating, fiery pain shoots along the fingers and up the arms to explode in the brain – the nails in the wrists are putting pressure on the median nerves. As he pushes himself upward to avoid stretching torment, he places the full weight on the nail through his feet. Again he feels the searing agony of the nail tearing through the nerves between the bones of the feet.

As the arms fatigue, cramps sweep through the muscles, knotting them in deep, relentless, throbbing pain. With those cramps comes the inability to push himself upward to breathe. Air can be drawn into the lungs but not exhaled. He fights to raise himself in order to get even one small breath. Finally carbon dioxide builds up in the lungs and in the blood stream, and the cramps partially subside. Spasmodically he is able to push himself upward to exhale and bring in life-giving oxygen.

Then he has to endure hours of limitless pain, cycles of twisting, joint-rending cramps, intermittent partial asphyxiation, searing pain as tissue is torn from his lacerated back as he moves up and down against the rough timber. Then another agony begins: a deep, crushing pain deep in the chest as the pericardium slowly fills with serum and begins to compress the heart.

It is now almost over – the loss of tissue fluids has reached a critical level – the compressed heart is struggling to pump heavy, thick, sluggish blood into the tissues – the tortured lungs are making a frantic effort to gasp in small gulps of air.

He can feel the chill of death creeping through his tissues... finally he can allow his body to die.

NOTES

1. O. Henry, 'A Retrieved Reformation', first published in *The Cosmopolitan Magazine* April 1903.

2. See for example Psalm 22.

3. Isaiah 52:13 – 53:12

4. See for example, Zechariah 11:12 and Matthew 26:15; 27:3; or Psalm 34:20 and John 19:33; or Zechariah 12:10 and John 19:34.

5. Mark 10:32–34.

6. 1 Corinthians 2:2, KJV.

7. Taken from *The Expositer's Bible Commentary* (Grand Rapids: Zondervan)

20

Have you seriously considered the weight of evidence for the resurrection of Jesus?

As Lord Chancellor in the nineteenth century, Lord Lyndhurst held the highest judicial office in the UK and was both a skilled lawyer and legislator. He said: 'I know pretty well what evidence is; and I tell you, such evidence as that for the Resurrection [of Jesus Christ] has never broken down yet.' [1]

Also speaking of Jesus' resurrection, Privy Councillor Charles Darling, who deputised for the Lord Chief Justice during World War One, said, '. . . there exists such overwhelming evidence, positive and negative, factual and circumstantial, that no intelligent jury in the world could fail to bring in a verdict that the resurrection story is true.' [2]

General Lew Wallace (1827–1905) was an atheist

who, encouraged by fellow atheist and sceptic Robert Ingersoll, set out to write a book that would prove Christianity to be a myth. He perused and studied the leading books in Europe and America. During the course of researching his book, Wallace became convinced of the historical truth of the life, death and resurrection of Jesus, and literally fell to his knees and cried out, 'My Lord and my God!' Wallace changed the purpose of his book and went on to write *Ben-Hur: A Tale of the Christ*, which is considered one of the greatest English novels.

Professor Simon Greenleaf, law professor at Harvard University, was an expert on the law of evidence. He too was sceptical of Christianity and set out to disprove it. However, he came to the conclusion that according to the laws of legal evidence used in courts of law, the resurrection is one of the best attested facts of ancient history.

Pinchas Lapide, a German Jewish rabbi, examined the evidence for the resurrection of Jesus, and in his book *The Resurrection of Jesus: A Jewish Perspective*,[3] concluded: 'I accept the resurrection of Easter Sunday not as an invention of the community of disciples, but as a historical event.'

The resurrection of Jesus is a vital part of the Christian message. It proves that Jesus is more than mere man; rather, He has power over death and the grave. As well, it demonstrates that He really did fully pay the price of people's sin, and that by raising Jesus from the dead, God was saying to this world that He had accepted the payment which Jesus had made for our sins.

It proves, too, that there is life after death. People sometimes say that no one has come back from the dead to tell us. But actually, someone has – Jesus rose again from the dead. That means that there will be a judgement for every human being. The first-century Christian, Paul, said to a group of philosophers in Athens, that God 'has appointed a day on which He will judge the world in righteousness by the Man whom He has ordained. He has given assurance of this to all by raising Him from the dead.' [4]

If Jesus rose again from the dead, He is unique in all the world religions: Mohammed, Buddha, Confucius, the popes have all died and been buried. Only Jesus rose, leaving an empty tomb.

So, what is the evidence?

Friends and foes of Christianity are agreed that Jesus lived, died and that the tomb in which He was buried was empty. We know these three facts from both the Bible and non-biblical records.

The Old Testament (the part of the Bible written long before Jesus) prophesied that the Messiah, the Holy One, would be born in Bethlehem, would live His life, would suffer and die, but that He would not 'see corruption'.[5] The New Testament documents describe the life Jesus lived and the death He died. The four Gospels, Matthew, Mark, Luke and John, record that Jesus' tomb was empty. Luke, a doctor who recorded the visit of the women to the tomb of Jesus on the first Easter Sunday morning, states, 'Then they went in and did not find the body of the Lord Jesus' (24:3, NKJV).

In contrast to other ancient manuscripts, there are thousands of copies (over twenty-four thousand) which date back to very shortly after they were originally written (the earliest written around AD130). Professor F.F. Bruce, previous Rylands professor of Biblical Criticism and Exegesis at the University of Manchester, stated that 'there is no body of ancient literature in the world which enjoys such a wealth of good textual attestation as the New Testament'.[6]

The New Testament is not the only source of evidence. Roman historians, Pliny the Younger,[7] Cornelius Tacitus [8] and Suetonius [9] each write of Jesus and His death. The Jewish historian, Josephus, who was born at the time of Jesus death, wrote:

Now there was about this time Jesus, a wise man, if it be lawful to call Him a man; for He was a doer of wonderful work, a teacher of such men as receive the truth with pleasure. He drew over to Him both many of the Jews and many of the Gentiles. He was [the] Christ. And when

Pilate, at the suggestion of the principal men amongst us, had condemned Him to the cross, those that loved Him at the first did not forsake Him; for He appeared to them alive again the third day; as the divine prophets had foretold these and ten thousand other wonderful things concerning Him. And the tribe of Christians, so named from Him, are not extinct at this day. [10]

The issue is not *whether* the tomb of Jesus was empty, but *why* it was empty. So, look at the five possibilities for which people have argued:

1. There was a mistake – perhaps the women and others went to the wrong tomb

However, the Bible records that the women clearly noted where the body of Jesus was buried. In fact, the original word used in the Bible to describe what Mary Magdalene and Mary the mother of Jesus did, translated, means that they took a 'good, long look at' the place. They remembered where their loved one was buried.

The tomb was also visited by Jesus' disciples, Peter and John. Moreover, they saw the discarded grave clothes. Did they go to the wrong tomb too?

Remember that followers of Jesus were really upsetting the status quo of both Jewish life and the Roman authorities by saying that Jesus had risen from the dead. Had the body of Jesus been in the tomb they would easily have been able to disprove the Christian claims that Jesus had risen from the dead by simply producing the body. But they couldn't. He was not there!

2. It was a delusion – perhaps the disciples saw a ghost, a hallucination or an apparition

Significantly, different types of people saw the risen Jesus. Matthew was a hard-headed tax collector; Peter was a tough fisherman; Paul was an intellectual academic; Thomas the sceptic has gone down in history as a doubter; Mary had just recently witnessed a triple crucifixion. They saw Him in different circumstances over a period of forty days: in a garden, on a mountain, in a room, on a road and by the seashore. On one occasion, He was seen by a crowd of over five hundred.

'BEHOLD MY HANDS AND MY FEET, THAT IT IS I MYSELF'

What was it that convinced ordinary, down-to-earth people that Jesus was risen? When some suspected that maybe Jesus was a spirit, He replied, 'Behold my hands and my feet, that it is I Myself. Handle me and see, for a spirit does not have flesh and bones as you see I have.' [11]

If these were merely hallucinations, why did they abruptly stop after forty days? And why did the authorities not produce the body of Jesus? That would have silenced the Christians who were boldly proclaiming the risen, living Jesus.

3. This was a fraud — the disciples stole the body

This is the oldest theory to explain away the resurrection, for the first suggestion of fraud is recorded in Matthew's Gospel. There we read that the Chief Priests and Pharisees made a request to Pilate, saying:

> we remember that while He was still alive that deceiver said, 'After three days I will rise again.' So give the order for the tomb to be made secure until the third day. Otherwise, His disciples may come and steal the body and tell the people that He has been raised from the dead. The last deception will be worse than the first. [12]

We then read that

> some of the guards went into the city and reported to the Chief Priests everything that had happened. When the Chief Priests had met with the elders and devised a plan, they gave the soldiers a large sum of money, telling them, 'You are to say, "His disciples came during the night and stole Him away while we were asleep." If this report gets to the governor, we will satisfy him and keep you out of trouble.' So the soldiers took the money and did as they were instructed. [13]

It really was a desperate explanation, because it was known that there were numerous security precautions set up. The tomb was guarded by soldiers. If they were Roman soldiers, they came as a highly disciplined four to sixteen-man security unit. If I had been a barrister in a court of law hearing that the soldiers said the body was stolen while they were sleeping, I would have asked the obvious question as to how they knew that if they were asleep.

As well, there was a heavy stone rolled in front of the tomb, and sealed. Jews treated bodies with great respect, so the dead body of Jesus was laden with aromatic spices before being carefully wrapped with linen cloths, separately around His body and His head. (There was not a complete sheet, so the idea of the Turin Shroud is shown to be untrue from a snippet of information which John's Gospel gives us in 20:6,7.)

Are we to believe that the hugely disappointed disciples somehow sneaked past the guards, moved the stone, carefully unwrapped the cloths around Jesus' body, neatly leaving them looking as if a body was still in place, and then removed the body of Jesus, carrying this naked corpse through the streets? And to where did they take it? What would they have done with the body? And what was their motive? Then, who was it who went around with nail wounds in His hands and

WHAT WOULD THEY HAVE DONE WITH THE BODY? AND WHAT WAS THEIR MOTIVE?

feet, looking and sounding like Jesus, convincing even the most sceptical that He was Jesus, risen from the dead? And would such deceivers have preached such good morality, then been willing to die for what they knew to be a fraud and deception? It is one thing to die for a passionately held illusion, but a very different thing to die for something you *know* to be a lie.

Chuck Colson was Special Counsel to President Nixon at the time of the Watergate scandal which rocked the United States. At the centre of the incident was a break-in to the Democratic Party headquarters. Twelve of the cleverest men believed they could cover up this and other associated crimes. Within three weeks, the truth had come out. Colson stated, 'Watergate embroiled twelve of the most powerful men in the world – and they couldn't keep a lie for three weeks. You're telling me twelve apostles could keep a lie for 40 years. Absolutely impossible!' [14]

> YOU'RE TELLING ME TWELVE APOSTLES COULD KEEP A LIE FOR 40 YEARS. ABSOLUTELY IMPOSSIBLE!

Rather, we read that when disciples of Jesus, Peter and John, went to the tomb where Jesus had been laid, they observed that the body had gone though the grave clothes remained. Peering at the place where Jesus' body had lain, they saw the cloths in the form of a body looking like an empty chrysalis of a caterpillar cocoon. John, the author of the Gospel, says of himself that he saw and believed.

4. Maybe Jesus merely swooned on the cross – He never actually died

Conceding that the tomb was empty and that the body of Jesus had gone and that He was appearing to people, it was first suggested by the German atheist Venturini that Jesus had simply fainted, to recover later when He was in the tomb.

Again, though the argument seems plausible initially, it totally ignores the facts that after being flogged in the most inhumane way with a Roman flagellum, a many-thonged whip (which Mel Gibson tried to portray in his film, *The Passion of the Christ*), nails were driven through Jesus' hands and feet as He was crucified. Hours later a spear was thrust into His side by a Roman soldier. John, an eyewitness, recalled the sight, 'But one of the soldiers pierced His side with a spear, and immediately blood and water came out.' [15] (Medically, upon death where there is heart failure, the sac around the heart called the pericardium becomes distended with serum – a watery fluid. The perforation of the sac, and the resultant flow of blood and serum was thus evidence that death had occurred.)

Jesus' body was then taken down, tightly bound in yards of linen grave clothes, weighed down by pounds of spice, and placed in a cold rock-hewn tomb in Jerusalem without food or water.

Are we then asked to believe that He regained sufficient strength not only to get on to His feet, but to undo the wrappings (and then fold them again leaving them as if there were still a body within them), break the seal which held (what was probably) the two-tonne stone in place at the mouth of the sepulchre, roll away the stone, walk eight miles on wounded feet, and then appear to the disciples in such splendour that they were convinced He was the risen, triumphant Christ?

5. Or, this was a miracle – Jesus did what He said He would

At dawn, on the first day of the week, Mary Magdalene and the other Mary went to look at the tomb. They discovered it was empty because Jesus had risen. They heard the words reverberate, 'He is not here; he has risen' [16]

Over the next forty days, Jesus appeared many times and in different circumstances, so that over five hundred and twenty people had seen the risen Christ. Most of these were alive at the time of writing the accounts of His resurrection and could testify to the truth of what they had seen and heard. He appeared five times on the day of His resurrection, first to Mary Magdalene and then to Mary the mother of James, Joanna and others as they hurried back to Jerusalem. Peter then met Jesus and was convinced, even after his three-fold denial of even knowing Jesus before the crucifixion. Cleopas and his companion met Jesus on the road to Emmaus in the late afternoon. Finally, Jesus appeared to the disciples in the Upper Room and had supper with them.

Illusionist Todd Alexander,[17] in one of his performances demonstrates how Jesus' resurrection cannot have been illusion. Interestingly, the three highest senses were involved in verifying the facts of the resurrection. Eyewitnesses saw and heard Jesus, and some were invited to touch him. This was no conjuring trick. Remember too that some who believed were initially sceptical or disbelieving – think of Thomas who said he would not believe unless he could put his fingers in the wounds of Jesus' hands, feet and side. As soon as Jesus appeared, Thomas fell on his knees, saying, 'My Lord and God!'[18] Saul of Tarsus was persecuting Christians until he was confronted by the risen Jesus, which turned him completely around.

EYEWITNESSES SAW AND HEARD JESUS, AND SOME WERE INVITED TO TOUCH HIM. THIS WAS NO CONJURING TRICK

Link this eyewitness evidence with the circumstantial evidence and the case seems watertight:

- The tomb where Jesus was laid was empty.

- The Roman seal on the stone was broken.

- The extremely large stone, which two people said

they could not move, had rolled away even though soldiers stood guard.

- A highly disciplined Roman military guard (some of whom fled when Jesus rose) had to be bribed to lie about what happened.

- The undisturbed grave clothes no longer contained the body.

- Christians began to worship not on their Saturday Sabbath but on the first day of the week to commemorate Jesus' resurrection.

- Early Christians willingly died testifying to the truth of Jesus' death and resurrection.

It is no wonder that Thomas Arnold, professor of Modern History at Oxford University said, 'I know of no one fact in the history of mankind which is proved by better and fuller evidence of every sort, to the understanding of a fair inquirer, than the great sign which God has given us that Christ died and rose again from the dead.' [19]

Frank Morison, a journalist, thought the resurrection was nothing more than a fairy tale happy ending. He set out to disprove it. Upon studying the facts, he came to a different conclusion. He wrote the bestselling book, *Who Moved the Stone?*, the first chapter of which was called 'The book that refused to be written'.

I remember asking my agnostic professor of Sociology if he had ever read the book. He had, and called it 'the most convincing piece of Christian literature I have ever read'. When I pressed him, he admitted he could not answer or explain it, but still would not believe in Jesus!

At the end of a law case, often a jury is called upon by the trial judge to deliver a verdict. The evidence for the resurrection demands a verdict from us. It seems intellectually dishonest to walk out on Jesus when the evidence for His life, death and resurrection is so overwhelming. Jesus said to Thomas, who believed only *after* seeing the risen Christ, 'Blessed are those who have not seen and yet have believed.' [20]

NOTES

1. *Who Moved the Stone?* (Milton Keynes: Authentic 2006), pp.9,10

2. www.knowtruth.com (accessed 21 May 2013).

3. Pinchas Lapide, trs. Wilhelm C. Lines *The Resurrection of Jesus: A Jewish Perspective* (London: SPCK, 1984).

4. Acts 17:31, NKJV.

5. See for example Psalm 16:10, Acts 2:27,31,Acts 13:35, NKJV.

6. http://www.angelfire.com/sc3/myredeemer/Evidencep7.html (accessed 7 August 2013)

7. Pliny, *Epistulae* Book 10, Letter 96.

8. Tacitus, *Annals* XV:44

9. Seutonius, *The Lives of the Caesars: The Life of Claudius* XXV:4.

10. Josephus, *Antiquities of the Jews* XVIII 3:3.

11. Luke 24:39, NKJV.

12. Matthew 27:63,64.

13. Matthew 28:11–15.

14. http://www.alwaysbeready.com/index.php/component/content/article/1-latest/241-apologetic-quote-charles-colson (accessed 7 August 2013)

15. John 19:34, KJV.

16. Matthew 28:6.

17. See www.illusion2reality.org (accessed 17 May 2013).

18. John 20:28.

19. See http://historicalapologetics.org/thomas-arnold-i-know-of-no-one-fact-in-the-history-of-mankind/ (accessed 17 May 2013).

20. John 20:29, NKJV.

21

Why are human beings so incurably religious?

When God created humans, He gave us a spiritual nature so that we would not only have an awareness that God exists, but that we might know Him personally. We were made to know God in an intimate, dynamic, growing way. The tragedy of sin is that it has made us dead to God and to the enjoyment of spiritual life. We know there is more to our life than millions of chemicals covered with skin that exists for three score years and ten, but it seems that the God who is there appears distant.

Animals give no evidence of being worshipping creatures, but wherever you go in the world, human beings worship. Their worship may be perverse or even perverted, but nevertheless it is a characteristic of all men and women that they want to worship.

In many Western nations, worship has been diverted from God to sport, celebrities, sex, self or sensuality.

Nevertheless, something within a human being wants to worship. From where does this desire come?

Trevor Knight was for many years the UK director of the inter-church youth movement, Young Life. He was an unforgettable speaker, and while preaching at an open air meeting in the centre of Nottingham a familiar atheist heckled him with the words, 'I've been an atheist for eighty-four years...' Trevor asked him his age, to which he replied 96, 'and I've been an atheist for eighty-four years!' Trevor retorted, 'Well, that shows you weren't born an atheist...'

We worship God not because He is egotistical and we are subservient scum. Rather, with a sense of awe, gratitude and overwhelming love, we delight to tell and show our Maker and Saviour how much He means to us. If Christians could not express this worship they would burst, because praise is the inevitable outcome of knowing God.

PRAISE IS THE INEVITABLE OUTCOME OF KNOWING GOD

Before becoming Christians, people sense the need to worship, but because sins have separated them from God, they hardly know how to. That is why Jesus came into the world. He said: 'the Son of Man has come to seek and to save that which was lost.' [1] Having lived a sinless life in perfect harmony with His Father, He set His face to go to Jerusalem where He would be crucified. While suffering more than we can imagine,

Jesus took on Himself the sin of all humankind, which had until then separated us from God. In so doing, He Himself was cut off from His Father in those hours on the cross. He was overwhelmingly tormented spiritually, as well as physically. He gave Himself so that we could be forgiven and reconciled to God. This supreme act of sacrifice on our behalf inspires us to worship. This is the great privilege of the Christian. We can know God in such a real way that we want to worship Him who loved us and gave Himself for us.

NOTE

1. Luke 19:10, NKJV.

22

Have you ever tried reading the Bible?

King George V said that 'the English Bible is the first of our national treasures'. Yet because it is a big book – in fact the one volume is a collection of 66 books, 39 in the Old Testament and 27 in the New Testament – it appears too daunting to attempt to read. In the Bible there is history, poetry, law, wisdom, prophecy and biography. Both the Old Testament – written before Jesus' life – and the New Testament focus on Jesus. The Old Testament, through pictures and prophecy, portray the Jesus who was yet to come. The New Testament tells us about Him, His life, work, teachings, death, resurrection, influence and power, and His return one day as Lord, King and Ruler on the earth.

French philosopher and novelist Jean-Jacques Rousseau (1712–78) said, 'I must confess to you that the majesty of the Scriptures astonishes me' and 'How petty are the books of philosophers, with all their pomp, compared with the Gospels!' The four Gospels are a good place to begin reading the Bible. Let Jesus introduce Himself to you; discover Him not as the Jesus of the RE lesson or the television programme, but the real Jesus. His words and works are startling. If you feel able, ask God to speak to you through His word. Then read on in the New Testament, discovering the truths which have changed individuals, nations and empires. When you open the pages of the Bible and read, it is as if you are opening the lips of God and allowing Him to speak to you. If you read in that way, God will honour your open attitude and stir up faith in your mind and heart.

23

From where do you get your moral compass?

Every society and individual needs rules of conduct, but is there an absolute standard of right and wrong? If so, from where does it come? If not, where is the line drawn between that which is good and that which is evil?

There are those who argue that there is no such thing as evil, but clearly they have never experienced a war zone or stood with the parents of a murdered child or if they have, they are lacking in simple human compassion and understanding.

Plato, long ago, posed the question: 'Are actions wrong because they are forbidden, or are they forbidden because they are wrong?' But he was assuming that there is right and wrong, so again we want to know the source of morality. Philosopher Immanuel Kant argued that absolutes are seen less as God's commands than as rules that humans understand through reason to be universally commendable. He argued that there are rules that go beyond our personal preferences so that they become a matter of duty.

However, duty and commands, if not given by an authoritative figure, can be changed. To take one compelling example, since parliament in 1967 legalised abortion in England and Wales, more unborn babies have been aborted than the number of Jews who died in the Holocaust. Someone has said that the least safe place to be in the UK is in a mother's womb. There is a dictum that morality consists in causing no harm to anyone. But it is of little value when our own rights are under threat. Situational ethics reflect whims, but do not set a standard of right and wrong. Others have said that virtue or love are the absolutes, but they need defining, and without absolute morality they will be adjusted according to our own desires, as we have seen in legislation in recent decades.

For the Christian, God Himself is the absolute. He is morally good and pure, just and merciful, unable to sin or speak untruth. He is holy – that is, set apart – and yet approachable. His character has been revealed and reflected in His commandments. They not only show us what is right, but reveal to us that we are so often wrong. The motive, though, is not to send us down a cul-de-sac of guilt, but to act as a schoolteacher leading us to Himself and the forgiveness that He offers. A Christian who has asked Jesus, by His Holy Spirit, to

HE IS HOLY – THAT IS, SET APART – AND YET APPROACHABLE

fill their mind and being, has new desires to live for Jesus and follow in His ways. Morality comes from God and is absolute; any other source is shifting sand, reflecting what is convenient for the way we choose to live.

24

Would you be willing to consider the possibility that you may have been brainwashed against true Christianity?

We are very defensive when told that we do not have open minds. We resist even the possibility of the thought that we could have been brainwashed. Of course, we acknowledge we are all subject to pressures and ideas which we naturally absorb and imbibe. We cannot help living in the times that we do! Whereas in the past there may have been a Christian consensus, today that has been eroded and attacked. Consequently, it is inevitable that we will be subject to secular influences.

British law decrees that every child should have at least fifteen thousand hours of education. For the vast majority of children that is in state schools. And yet so many subjects taught have content which is directly contrary to biblical teaching. Even school assemblies and Religious Education lessons often act as inoculation against real Christianity. They can be lifeless teaching and yet, while treating most religions sympathetically, they undermine the foundation of Christian beliefs by deriding biblical teachings and morality. Education is a cousin of indoctrination, but directed towards people of deeply impressionable ages. We have become victims of this. In Higher Educational establishments, atheists are allowed to drip-feed their thoughts while, when it comes to sharing their faith, Christians are silenced and their jobs threatened. The same is happening in the workplace, particularly in public service; we know there have been many high-profile cases which have hit the headlines. [1] All this has its impact on our perceptions and ideas. It is no longer politically correct or expedient to adhere to or defend Christian beliefs.

WHEN IT COMES TO SHARING THEIR FAITH, CHRISTIANS ARE SILENCED AND THEIR JOBS THREATENED

The most all-pervasive influence is that of the broadcasters – though the BBC does not have a monopoly on television and radio, it is the most dominant. It has some great film-makers and photographers. It produces some wonderful programmes. Its sports coverage is ever-popular (even if many sports are overlooked).

Despite its biases, most people trust 'the Beeb' and we want it to do well.

The BBC is obliged by its charter to be impartial, and the BBC is committed to reflecting a diversity of opinion in all areas, including religion.

Its stated aims seem admirable. Sadly, its practice is very different. And a recent Director General of the BBC, Mark Thompson, admitted it when he argued that Jesus is 'fair game' because Christianity has broad shoulders and fewer ties to ethnicity. BBC news anchorman Peter Sissons also said Christians are 'fair game' for insults by the corporation because, he said, 'they do nothing about it if they are offended'. [2] These are important issues because we cannot help but be greatly influenced by the hours of listening to the media. But if it has an agenda which is against Christianity, it may be that we are absorbing its message, and thus being subtly brainwashed.

We know that the BBC regularly uses the words 'Jesus', 'Christ' and 'God' as blasphemy in their plays on radio and films on television. Its presenters incessantly criticise Christian beliefs and values; they very rarely have anyone on air who expresses traditional Christian beliefs. Christianity is treated like a 'freak show' and programmes are produced 'that have tended to look at the fringes of Christianity where it can be brought into disrepute' [3]

The BBC readily showed *Jerry Springer: The Opera* with its uninhibited blasphemy, despite over fifty thousand complaints about the programme. One cannot imagine them mocking any other religious leader like that; nor would one want them to. We remember that it was the BBC who didn't even want to play Cliff Richard's single 'The Lord's Prayer' some Christmases ago. A while back, they appointed an atheist as head of Religious Broadcasting, then replaced him with a Muslim.

It is right and proper to respect other people's beliefs and culture. But the BBC uses its influence to pedal secular humanism as its religion. Secularism is as much a religion as any other, but it is the backcloth philosophy to its regular output. One therefore has to question whether it is complying with its charter to be an impartial broadcaster.

When the BBC was discussing whether to include atheists as contributors to their 'Thought for the Day' on the Radio 4 *Today* programme, the atheist Rod Liddle wrote about it in *The Sunday Times*.[4] He said:

> *The BBC Trust is considering whether to open up* 'Thought for the Day' *to atheists. But the three-minute religious slot on* Today *is, in fact, secular already. God is almost never allowed to poke His nose into a broadcast, and when He does, it is with apologies, and embarrassment. He does no smiting, He is never angry, no matter what issues come before Him. The God you hear in* 'Thought for the

Day' has been created by BBC producers in their image – a slightly disappointed but nonetheless benevolent middle-aged man of confused sexuality who wishes that everybody might live together peaceably in a warm and caring multicultural society...

The BBC is brilliant at portraying and broadcasting life without God. Have you noticed how very many of the BBC anchors are atheists? And do you wonder what the BBC's reason is for this?

Even if the BBC kept to their stated aims, there is a problem. All religions are not the same, and indeed cannot all be true. Compare their beliefs about God: Hindus believe in a vast array of gods, Buddhists believe in none; Muslims and Jews believe in one God, as do Christians. But Christians believe that the one God is uniquely a Trinity of three persons: Father, Son and Holy Spirit. Clearly, they cannot all be right.

ALL RELIGIONS ARE NOT THE SAME, AND INDEED CANNOT ALL BE TRUE

The Christian doctrine of 'justification by faith' (that people are saved through faith in the finished work of Jesus in His death and resurrection) impacted the whole of Europe at the time of the Reformation. Countries in the north of the continent were radically transformed by that one belief. Today, millions rely on Christ and are 'justified by faith'. Yet the media rarely, if ever, carry that message.

Have you noticed that when Christians are interviewed, there is a strange silence about this crucial belief. BBC presenter Jeremy Vine said he believed it had become 'almost socially unacceptable to say you believe in God'.[5] Simon Mayo said religion is 'increasingly driven to the margin' of the BBC.[6]

The BBC portrays religion as humankind's long search for God. Christianity focuses on God's seeking for us. As humans, we were created to know God, but our wrongdoing, our sins, have cut us off from Him. There is an incompleteness, an emptiness within us all. Spiritually we are dead, yet we know there is something wrong. God has taken the initiative in coming to rescue us.

The truth is that while sometimes we would like to know God, we also run away from Him, and do our own thing. Instead of us searching for God, He has taken the initiative and come searching for us.

If you get the idea from the media that religion is all about rules, regulations and rituals, then you will be intrigued by reading in the Bible to see how Jesus spoke against such notions. Jesus taught that a person can know God in a personal way. He explained that God can be our Father and we may become His sons and daughters. Christianity is not about what we do, but what God has done for us.

GOD CAN BE OUR FATHER AND WE MAY BECOME HIS SONS AND DAUGHTERS

Of course, there are things that a real Christian will not want to do, and others things that become their lifestyle, but the essence of Christianity is about God reaching out to ordinary people so that He might bring us to Himself.

When Jesus was crucified, God was doing something remarkable. He took the guilt of each one of us and laid it on Jesus. He died carrying the can for our sin. It is impossible for us to finally pay the penalty for what we have done wrong but Jesus, the eternal One, paid for it all in three hours on the cross. Sadly, you will rarely, if ever, hear that message on radio or television, yet it is history's most significant moment. Jesus died so that we could be forgiven and reconciled to God.

On the first Easter Sunday morning, Jesus rose from the dead. We admire certain political and religious leaders of the past, but when they died they were buried or cremated. That was it. In contrast, Jesus rose from the dead, and is alive today. What we do with Jesus matters for eternity. Heaven is not for the good and hell for the bad, for no one deserves heaven. Rather, heaven is for those whose sin is forgiven; it is for those who have been made righteous (i.e. seen by God as covered in Jesus' goodness, even though we are still sinners) through what Jesus has done for them through His death and resurrection.

These issues are too important to get wrong. It would

be an awful thing to go through life and then into eternity and never know God. Don't get your religion from the BBC! Read the Bible for yourself. Read the four Gospels, the 'biographies' of Jesus. Let Him introduce Himself to you. The word of God lasts for ever and will be around long after individual broadcasters and even the BBC itself are forgotten.

NOTES

1. Look on the Christian Institute website for more information on these cases: www.christian.org.uk (accessed 17 May 2013).

2. See Christian Institute website for 29 February 2012 (accessed 17 May 2013).

3. See Christian Institute website for 22 June 2009 (accessed 17 May 2013).

4. *The Sunday Times* 20 July 2009.

5. See http://www.dailymail.co.uk/news/article-1121223/Why-I-won-8217-t-discuss-Christianity-air-Radio-2-Panorama-host-Jeremy-Vine.html (accessed 17 May 2013).

6. See http://www.telegraph.co.uk/culture/tvandradio/6951450/BBC-is-driving-religion-to-the-margins-says-Simon-Mayo.html (accessed 17 May 2013).

25

How do you explain how lives are radically changed when people put their trust in Jesus?

Conversion is not just the acceptance of a particular creed, but a change of heart. It involves a turning around: turning from our sin to God and His Son, Jesus. At conversion, God does a deep work in the mind and heart of the person, so that He who made us, remakes us. And He does this at great cost to Himself. It cost only words to bring everything into existence, but to convert us and bring us to Himself cost the life, the blood, the suffering of Jesus on the cross.

Famously, C.S. Lewis, author of the Narnia series of books and *Mere Christianity* (among others), recalls his conversion story:

> *You must picture me alone in that room... night after night, feeling, whenever my mind lifted even for a second*

from my work, the steady, unrelenting approach of Him whom I so earnestly desired not to meet. That which I greatly feared had at last come upon me. In the Trinity Term of 1929 I gave in, and admitted that God was God, and knelt and prayed: perhaps, that night, the most dejected and reluctant convert in all England... but who can duly adore that Love which will open the high gates to a prodigal who is brought in kicking, struggling, resentful, and darting his eyes in every direction for a chance to escape. [1]

When people ask Jesus to be their Lord and Saviour, not only is the past forgiven and the conscience cleared, but a new joy, peace and purpose starts to take a grip on them. For some, there is such a radical transformation that everyone can see they are completely new people. This is not just a passing phase, an enthusiasm, but as the Bible puts it, they have become new creations in Christ; the old has gone, the new has come. [2] When people become aware of God, their manner, demeanour, their vocabulary, their reactions and relationships turn around. What a power this is that changes people so clearly that the best way to describe them is that they have been born again!

Jesus spoke to a deeply religious Jewish leader and said that 'no one can see the kingdom of God unless they are born again'. [3] So Christian conversion is a must for all who will come to know God in life, through death, and into eternity.

Atheistic journalist and left-wing politician Roy Hattersley, writing in *The Guardian* (12 September 2005) just after Hurricane Katrina had caused severe damage in the USA, wrote challenging his own atheism. Below are extracts from his article:

The Salvation Army has been given a special status as provider-in-chief of American disaster relief. But its work is being augmented by all sorts of other groups. Almost all of them have a religious origin and character.

Notable by their absence are teams from rationalist societies, free thinkers' clubs and atheists' associations – the sort of people who not only scoff at religion's intellectual absurdity but also regard it as a positive force for evil.

Late at night, on the streets of one of our great cities, that man (a Salvation Army worker) offers friendship as well as help to the most degraded and (to those of a censorious turn of mind) degenerate human beings who exist just outside the boundaries of our society. And he does what he believes to be his Christian duty without the slightest suggestion of disapproval. Yet, for much of his time, he is meeting needs that result from conduct he regards as intrinsically wicked.

Civilised people do not believe that drug addiction and male prostitution offend against divine ordinance. But those who do are the men and women most willing to

change the fetid bandages, replace the sodden sleeping
bags and – probably most difficult of all – argue, without
a trace of impatience, that the time has come for some
serious medical treatment. Good works, John Wesley
insisted, are no guarantee of a place in Heaven. But they
are most likely to be performed by people who believe
that Heaven exists.

It ought to be possible to live a Christian life without
being a Christian or, better still, to take Christianity à la
carte... Yet men and women who, like me, cannot accept
the mysteries and the miracles do not go out with the
Salvation Army at night.

The only possible conclusion is that faith comes with
a packet of moral imperatives that, while they do not
condition the attitude of all believers, influence enough of
them to make them morally superior to atheists like me.

The truth may make us free. But it has not made us as
admirable as the average captain in the Salvation Army.

NOTES

1. C.S. Lewis, *Surprised by Joy* (London: Collins, 2012).
2. See 2 Corinthians 5:17.
3. John 3:3.

26

Why do you think Christians have always been at the forefront of social reform?

Atheist Jürgen Habermas, in *Time of Transitions* [1] said, 'Christianity, and nothing else, is the ultimate foundation of liberty, conscience, human rights and democracy, the benchmarks of Western civilization. To this day, we have no other options. We continue to nourish ourselves from this source.'

On both sides of the Atlantic and across the world, it was Christianity that gave us our universities, with the freedom to study, and the laws that protect the right to propagate people's views.

William Wilberforce went to parliament at the age of 21, as a self-seeking politician. Through the influence of brilliant Cambridge scholar Isaac Milner, Wilberforce asked Jesus Christ to become his Lord and Saviour. He put behind him the win-at-all-costs politics and devoted himself to serve Christ. He established schools for the deaf and blind, lending libraries, trade schools and colleges. He helped in the founding of the National Gallery and the RSPCA and funded scientific research, the distribution of Bibles and the preaching of the gospel of Jesus Christ. He was responsible for the abolition of the National Lottery of his day. He is most remembered for his work for the abolition of the slave trade throughout the British Empire. And the motivation for all these reforms was the transformation he experienced the moment he, as an MP, trusted Jesus Christ. He said that it was God who motivated him.

Similar stories can be told about the impact of Christian conversion on the lives of Dr Thomas Barnardo and George Müller, both responsible for the establishing of orphanages, and Elizabeth Fry and John Howard who brought about prison reform. Lord Shaftesbury, known as 'the friend of the poor', toured asylums showing compassion. He worked for the abolition of the use of children and half-naked women in hauling coal in mines. He legislated against child chimney sweeps, fed starving children and built new and better housing estates. Hundreds of thousands of mourners lined the streets at his funeral, knowing that 'the poor man's earl' had served the God He trusted, and for His sake, served the poor.

LORD SHAFTESBURY, KNOWN AS 'THE FRIEND OF THE POOR', TOURED ASYLUMS SHOWING COMPASSION

Henry Dunant, who founded the Red Cross, David Livingstone who was so loved in Africa, Florence Nightingale who served compassionately in the Crimean War, were each Christian people. Tens of thousands of others served and serve across the world, respecting others, caring for the underdogs of societies, sharing with them the good news of Jesus because He has done so much for them.

The Bible teaches that if anyone is 'in Christ' they become a new creation, the old life goes and a new life begins. [2] Jesus taught us to love those around us, even our enemies; Christians are commanded to care for the poor, the weak, widows and orphans. He said:

When the Son of Man comes in His glory, and all the angels with Him, He will sit on his throne in heavenly glory. All the nations will be gathered before Him, and He will separate the people one from another as a shepherd separates the sheep from the goats. He will put the sheep on His right and the goats on His left. Then the King will say to those on His right, 'Come, you who are blessed by my Father; take your inheritance, the kingdom prepared for you since the creation of the world. For I was hungry and you gave me something to eat, I was thirsty and you gave me something to drink, I was a stranger and you invited me in, I needed clothes and you clothed me, I was sick and you looked after me, I was in prison and you came to visit me.' Then the righteous will answer him, 'Lord, when did we see you hungry and feed you, or thirsty and give you something to drink? When did we see you a stranger and invite you in, or needing clothes and clothe you? When did we see you sick or in prison and go to visit you?' The King will reply, 'I tell you the truth, whatever you did for one of the least of these brothers of mine, you did for me.' [3]

Undoubtedly there have been – and are – kind and compassionate people who do not trust in Jesus, but it is He who changes the selfish and makes them selfless, who gives His heart of love to those who follow Him, and the power to do the work that He prepares for those who come to know Him personally.

NOTES

1. Jürgen Habermas, in *Time of Transitions* (Cambridge: Polity Press, 2006).
2. 2 Corinthians 5:17.
3. Matthew 25:31–40.

27

Have you noticed that real Christians are willing to forgive those who have hurt them?

Victor Hugo unforgettably illustrated kindness in his famous book, *Les Miserables*. It is only fiction, but Victor Hugo understood the power of kindness and forgiveness and recognised that these qualities characterise the Christian's life. The book is the story of Jean Valjean, whose only crime was the theft of a loaf of bread to feed his sister's starving children. After serving nineteen years in prison for his crime, he was released. Unable to find work because he had been a convict, he came to the home of a Christian bishop who kindly gave him some supper and a place to sleep. Yielding to temptation, however, Valjean stole the bishop's silver plates and slipped out into the night. But he was apprehended and brought back to the scene of the crime. The kind bishop did not want to prosecute the man, but wanted him to come to know the Lord, so told the officers he wanted Valjean to have the silver plates. Turning to the man, he said, 'And Jean, you forgot to take the candlesticks.' The criminal was astounded and the kindness later resulted in his transformation, bringing a deep sense of joy to the compassionate bishop.

Victor Hugo understood that forgiveness is at the heart of the Christian message. Christians are forgiven sinners. God never forgave an excuse, but if we are honest about our sin, confess it to Him and ask Jesus to forgive us, He does. One mark of that is that we then find that we can forgive others when they ask us. We are people who have put our trust in Jesus to wash away all past wrong, and find there is a new willingness to forgive those who harm us. We read this in the Lord's Prayer, where we pray, 'Forgive us our sins, as we forgive those who sin against us.'

VICTOR HUGO UNDERSTOOD THAT FORGIVENESS IS AT THE HEART OF THE CHRISTIAN MESSAGE

In January 2003 Robin Oake, Chief Constable of the Isle of Man, received a phone call to say that his son, Stephen, a detective constable with Special Branch, while on an anti-terror raid in Manchester had been murdered. Later Robin stunned a press conference by speaking of his willingness to forgive his son's murderer. He later reflected, 'I did mean it: I do mean it and I actually pray for the man who was convicted of Steve's killing every day, every morning when I get up.' The killer, Kamel Bourgass, an Algerian, has been jailed for life. Robin says that he believes forgiveness is possible in every situation of life where someone has been hurt or accused. He says, 'It's taken from us the bitterness and the anger that we might have had and we might still have... we've been healed from that.' [1]

God is a forgiving God who gives the strength and ability to Christians so that they, in turn, can forgive others as they have been forgiven.

NOTE

1. Robin Oake, *Father Forgive* (Milton Keynes: Authentic, 2008).

28

How would you define a Christian?

On 20 April 1999, in the small suburban town of Littleton, Colorado, two intelligent teenage boys from solid homes entered their school in the middle of the day with knives, guns and bombs. They planned to kill hundreds of their peers. By the end of the day twelve students, one teacher and the two murderers, Dylan Klebold and Eric Harris, were dead.

In trying to understand how such a massacre could have happened, many pointed the finger of blame at Dylan and Eric's parents for failing to bring them up well. Ten years after the event, Dylan's mother, Susan, said in Oprah Winfrey's magazine:

> In raising Dylan, I taught him how to protect himself from a host of dangers: lightning, snake bites, head injuries, skin cancer, smoking, drinking, sexually transmitted diseases, drug addiction, reckless driving, even carbon monoxide poisoning. It never occurred to me that the gravest danger – to him and, as it turned out, to so many others – might come from within.[1]

Thankfully, most of us are not going to become murderers. But what is it about human beings that, though we are so wonderfully made, amazingly intelligent and creative, we find ourselves living in a way that in our better moments appals us? We know the symptoms, but what is really wrong with us?

Jesus, who loved all types of people more than we can ever imagine, answered that question when He said, 'What comes out of you is what defiles you. For from within, out of your hearts, come evil thoughts, sexual immorality, theft, murder, adultery, greed, malice, deceit, lewdness, envy, slander, arrogance and folly. All these evils come from inside and defile you.' [2] We may argue that we are not guilty of any of these, but the potential is there because of our essential self-centredness. The opposite of this is selflessness – towards others, and towards God.

The claims of Christianity are of such significance that it makes sense for us all to take a closer look at Jesus, who He is and what He has done.

We were created amazing human beings, designed to enjoy the life God had given us and to know Him individually. But in a deliberate act of rebellion the first human beings defied God by disobeying Him, and brought into creation the sin which has wreaked havoc in our lives and world. Jesus' half-brother, James, wrote in the Bible, 'What is causing the quarrels and fights among you? Don't they come from the evil desires at war within you?' [3] We may not feel too bad, but our sin – the breaking of God's commandments – is serious. It cuts us off from God, will keep us out of heaven, and would condemn us to hell. The Bible is brutally frank when it teaches that all of us have sinned against God.

There is something strangely fascinating about the scandals in the lives of others. The fact that some celebrity is being exposed brings a wry smile to us, possibly because we are aware that we have been guilty of the same kind of misdemeanours, but no one would be interested in the details of our lives. Our greatest problem, according to the Bible, is that all of us have sinned against God.

There is another major problem that confronts us, which is the result of our having disobeying God. Like cut flowers, which bring so much pleasure for a while but soon wither, we too will one day die. Death is an unwelcome intruder into our lives and plans. The best of doctors, fitness programmes and vitamins all fail when the Grim Reaper approaches. Something inside us cries out that there must be an answer, otherwise life is meaningless.

David Mellor was a cabinet minister and is now a radio presenter. Recently at the Royal Society of Portrait Painters he said what many must feel, 'Everything I have done in life has been redundant. My life has been one exercise in futility.' Without God in a person's life, that is the rational conclusion.

If that was the sum total of the Christian message, we would have little reason to rejoice, and yet Christians are joyful people. It is not that they, like the ostrich, have buried their heads in the sand, but rather have faced the issue and found that God has the answer to their dilemma.

The hiding place

I love the story of the little girl who answered the phone only to hear the question, 'Is your father there?'

'Yes,' she whispered.

'Could I speak to him, please?'

'No. He's very busy,' the girl replied in a low voice.

'Well, is your mother there?'

'Yes. But she's very busy too.'

'Is anybody else there?'

Still whispering, the little girl answered, 'Yes, the police are here.'

'Then could I speak with a police officer please?'

'No. They're very busy as well.'

'Is anybody else there?' the caller asked, becoming exasperated.

'Yes, the fire brigade are here. But they're busy too.'

'What's going on, with so many people there and everybody busy?'

Innocently but quietly she replied, 'They're all looking for me!'

Hiding is a childish adventure, in which we have all been involved. It can be quite exciting. But to be on the run from our Maker and God is a different matter altogether. The stark fact is that we have not only run from God, but rebelled against Him with our wrong thoughts, words and actions. Our sins and evil deeds have separated us from the altogether good God.

It is strangely perverse that though God has given us our lives, we want to turn from Him, to ignore Him. God has revealed to us who He is and what He is like. He is spirit; we cannot touch or see Him. God knows all things and can do everything. He is everywhere and so sees us running from Him. He is absolutely pure, just, loving, reliable and unchanging.

The message of the Bible is that in His compassion towards us, He has come looking for us. There is only one God, who is Father, Son and Holy Spirit. He is a personal and relational God. We have become strange creatures when we prefer our dark ways to God's light and life and love. God is eternal, with no beginning or end. And the Father sent the Son to be the Saviour of the

THERE IS ONLY ONE GOD, WHO IS FATHER, SON AND HOLY SPIRIT

world. Having gone our own way, Jesus came to bring us back into a relationship with God Himself.

Jesus said of His mission, '[I have come] to seek and save those who are lost' [4] and 'For even [I] came not to be served but to serve others and to give [my] life as a ransom for many.' [5]

Nowadays, ransom is essentially a payment demanded for the release of kidnap victims. Once in a while we hear of a demand for ransom. For instance, Somali pirates have become experts in this practice. Celebrities can be targets. Frank Sinatra Jnr, Eric Peugeot (son of the car manufacturer) and John Paul Getty III were each redeemed with millions of pounds after having been kidnapped as children. But Jesus' ransom was profoundly different. He gave His life to release us from our enslavement to sin, and enable us to be reunited with His Father.

Husband buys back his wife!

Hosea lived 2,700 years ago. He was a well-known preacher in his community. When he announced he was to marry, you can imagine that it was the talk of the town. God had guided him to marry a woman called Gomer. Every detail of their lives would have been scrutinised. In time, they had a son and daughter, but then disaster struck, which would have been hard for the ordinary onlooker to believe. Gomer walked out on Hosea to become a prostitute. It was totally humiliating to Hosea, but it was to be an illustration of a great truth.

In time God instructed Hosea to go, find and then buy back his wife, who was being sold as a slave. Imagine some of the places he had to search to locate her – and he was a prophet! He eventually found his wife in the marketplace, about to be auctioned off. Hosea stood in the crowd and with silver and barley outbid everyone else. He redeemed his wife. She was his by right, and he was hers – they were married; but now she was doubly his. She had been redeemed at a great price.

SHE HAD BEEN REDEEMED AT A GREAT PRICE

In the heartache of the story of Hosea is an illustration of a great truth. Like Gomer, the nation of Israel (as well as us today) had sold themselves to do wrong: to live with little thought of God. Hosea did what God was eventually going to do; that is, to buy back what was rightfully His. For Hosea, the price was great; for God, the price to redeem us was greater still.

The Bible is God's written message to humanity. It reveals Him to us. It describes the marvellous moment in history when God took on Himself a human body and made His dwelling among us. Like two musical keys on a piano being played at the same moment and blending into one chord, so the nature of God and man perfectly blended in the person of Jesus Christ. He was fully God and fully human.

Jesus was God, taking the initiative in coming to reach, rescue and redeem us. He came to buy and bring us back to God, but euros, pounds or dollars could never be a sufficient price for that. The price that Jesus paid was His own blood.

Peter, the disciple of Jesus, wrote to Christians in different parts of the world saying, 'you were not redeemed with corruptible things, like silver or gold, from your aimless conduct received by tradition from your fathers, but with the precious blood of Christ...' [6]

Paul, who wrote many of the books in the New Testament part of the Bible, said, '. . . in [Jesus] we have redemption through His blood, the forgiveness of sins, according to the riches of His grace which He made to abound toward us...' [7]

The ransom paid

Most religions of the world tell us to try our best and work our way to God. But are we really to believe that any human being could be good enough to impress God, who is unapproachably pure? The Bible tells us that God is too great and holy for small, sinful humans to reach. Yet God, in His immense love, has come for us.

He has not dismissed us, but neither has He overlooked

the guilt of our lives. In Jesus, God has provided a costly ransom to deal with our sin and to buy us back into the relationship with Him for which we were created. Our sin is not only wrongful actions, thoughts and words, but also right actions which we have failed to take.

All the headline-hitting crimes of the world, as well as the hidden sins of the ordinary millions of men and women who simply go about their lives unnoticed by others, were laid on Jesus when He was crucified at Calvary. He, the eternal One, 'carried the can' for our sin. He died, was buried in a cave, and three days later rose again.

Through the death and resurrection of Jesus we can have forgiveness, freedom and a forever relationship with God. Jesus will bring us to know God, as we trust Him to be our Lord and Saviour.

This totally transforms our attitude to everything that life presents to us. The Holy Spirit of God comes to actually live within the lives of those who trust Jesus. The eighteenth-century preacher, John Wesley, said of fellow Christians, 'The best of all is, God is with us'. That is what Jesus promised. He is there as a friend both through the good and tough times of life. The Bible says, 'For [God] Himself has

THE HOLY SPIRIT OF GOD COMES TO ACTUALLY LIVE WITHIN THE LIVES OF THOSE WHO TRUST JESUS

said, "I will never leave you nor forsake you." So we may boldly say: "The LORD is my helper; I will not fear. What can man do to me?"'[8]

A story from the West... and from the East

Uncle Tom's Cabin was the bestselling novel of the nineteenth century. Written by Harriet Beecher Stowe, it tells the story of a longsuffering black slave called Tom, who is sold by his owner in Kentucky to pay off his debts. Eventually Tom is sold again to a cruel cotton plantation owner, who one day beats him to within an inch of his life. Belatedly, the son of Tom's first master arrives to redeem Tom. He finds him lying in a shed and pleads, 'You shan't die! You mustn't die, nor think of it. I've come to buy you and take you home.'

Tom's reply is potent: 'O Mas'r George, ye're too late. The Lord's bought me, and is going to take me home – and I long to go. Heaven is better than Kintuck.'[9]

But that is fiction. In real life, a man named Job lived centuries ago in the East. He was devout and well respected in his community – until his world collapsed around him. Within days, each of his children died in freak incidents, his business collapsed and he was wracked with numerous illnesses. Neither he nor those who tried to comfort him understood what was happening. And yet in that dire suffering he trusted in God. He said, 'I know that my Redeemer lives, and that in the end he will stand upon the earth. And after my skin has been destroyed, yet in my flesh I will see God; I myself will see him with my own eyes – I, and not another.' [10]

Job lived long before Jesus, but just as we look back to Christ, Job looked forward to the time when Jesus would come. He was confident, certain even, that one day God would rule over all creation.

No one relishes the idea of suffering or death. Christians, though, have a confidence that Jesus, their Redeemer, will be with them throughout life, through death, and into eternity. It is not that they are good enough for God and heaven – nobody is – but rather that all which would condemn them has been forgiven. Heaven is not a reward; it is a gift. The Bible says, 'For the wages of sin is death, but the gift of God is eternal life in Christ Jesus our Lord.' [11] Christians are people who have been made right with God when they turned from their sin, and trusted Jesus to be their Redeemer – their Lord, Saviour and Friend. They have found that Jesus is the answer to the problems of sin, death and meaninglessness.

Would you be willing to trust Jesus in this way? Are you longing that Jesus, the Redeemer, would now bring you to know God? Do you want to put your trust in Jesus and receive Him as Lord of your life?

I took a closer look

I was converted to Christ when I was 15 years of age. I was on holiday in the Middle East where a relative, who worked as a Christian minister, explained the good news of Jesus to me. He asked me if I had ever trusted Jesus Christ in this way. Clearly I hadn't, but I knew that I wanted to. He explained to me that following Jesus can be tough but I simply felt that if Jesus had died for me, then I must trust Him.

That very day, sitting on a log on the mountains of the Lebanon, I prayed asking Jesus to become my Lord and Saviour as I committed my life to Him. I have never regretted that moment. There was no flash in the sky, but neither was it a flash in the pan. The greatest joy of my life has been to live it with Christ as my Redeemer. I encourage you too to trust Him in this way.

NOTES

1. *O, The Oprah Magazine*, 13 October 2009.
2. Mark 7:20–23, TNIV.
3. James 4:1, NLT.
4. Luke 19:10, NLT.
5. Mark 10:45, NLT.
6. 1 Peter 1:18,19, NKJV.
7. Ephesians 1:7,8, NKJV.
8. Hebrews 13:5,6, NKJV.
9. Harriet Beecher Stowe, *Uncle Tom's Cabin* (Ware: Wordsworth Editions Ltd, 1999).
10. Job 19:25–27.
11. Romans 6:23..

29

Is your view of 'church' how church really is?

I have been to church services, looked around, and thought that I don't understand why these people are here, but fully understand why so many others are not. I have been to school 'chapel' services which are dire. (Just as English lessons at school put me off Shakespeare, so RE lessons thoroughly turned me off religion.) However, at the conclusion of the very latest church service I attended, the gentleman in the seat next to me turned at the end and emphatically remarked, 'I enjoyed that!' I replied with equal emphasis, 'So did I!'

Church can be great. I look forward to each Sunday service. I would encourage every one to try church, but there are some vital things to look for. Sadly, the history of the church is that there has been a tendency for churches to drift away from the authority of the Bible, replacing it with traditions and the preaching of morality or politics rather than the word of God. That partly explains why there are so many denominations, though of course, they inevitably reflect personal preferences for the type of worship which suits individuals.

Find a church where the Bible is unconditionally believed and preached, where Jesus is worshipped and followed, and where the Christians genuinely care for one another, praying and serving together, and you will see that, though not perfect, there is integrity and a heartfelt reverence towards God the Father, the Son and the Holy Spirit. There is nothing to compare with a Christian church which is sincerely trusting in the living God and experiencing Him at work in their lives and community. I have found this to be true in small village churches and in large city churches, and in churches in the various parts of the world where I have had the privilege of travelling.

Of course, the church is a community of forgiven sinners, so there are always going to be issues. As in a hospital where there are going to be sick people, so in a church the collection of sinners (that's all of us) is at times going to test one's patience.

But then by joining, we ourselves only add to the problem! One of the evidences of true Christian conversion is that the Christian wants to go to church and be with other believers. It can be challenging, and needs discipline. I go twice each Sunday, not to earn favours from God – that would

OF COURSE, THE CHURCH IS A COMMUNITY OF FORGIVEN SINNERS

never work – but because He has shown His favour to me in forgiving me and bringing me into a relationship with Himself. I, for one, usually find church a little taster of heaven. I love it, and find it sets me up for facing the week ahead.

30

Have you wondered why Christians have been persecuted through the last twenty centuries?

There are very many parts of the world where people who desire to worship have been – or are increasingly being – brutally suppressed by imprisonment or execution. Often simply to be known to be a Christian is perilous. Communist countries in Europe and the Far East have been guilty of this. In the years before 1989, I had the privilege of working with Christians in some of these countries who dared to risk everything to worship with other Christians, and saw their total commitment to Jesus. North Korea, China, Vietnam and Cuba are only four of over forty countries where this persecution and pressure continues.

In most Islamic countries of the Middle East, persecution is routine for anyone who dares to worship any God other than Allah. We know of countries where the persecution is brutal and where 'apostasy' as they call it can result in a sentence of death. But the persecution of followers of Jesus is nothing new.

John the Baptist, the cousin of Jesus, was the last of the prophets to herald the arrival of the Messiah (Jesus). John pointed Him out to the crowds, describing Him as 'the Lamb of God, who takes away the sin of the world'. [1] But when John spoke out against the marriage of King Herod to his brother's wife, the king had him beheaded.

Part of the history of Christianity is the story of individual Christians laying down their lives rather than denying Jesus, who laid down His life for them. The countries that make up the United Kingdom have had their share of men and women who died because of their faith, and martyrs' memorials around the country bear testimony to their life and death.

That may seem very distant to us today, but it has been reckoned that there were more Christian martyrs in the twentieth century than in all the preceding centuries added together. Communism and Islam have been particularly, though not exclusively, guilty of persecution against the followers of Jesus. In the very last year of the last millennium, 1999, Graham, Philip and Timothy Staines, a father and two sons were burnt to death in Orissa, India. Graham, an Australian, had worked for thirty-five years caring for leprosy victims and translating the Bible into the Ho tribal language. One night, while they were sleeping in their Jeep, a militant Hindu who hated Christ took a group and set fire to the Jeep. Graham's widow, Gladys, and their daughter have stayed in India and are continuing the work amongst leprosy patients. Gladys said, 'How was I able to forgive? The truth is that I myself am a sinner. I needed Jesus Christ to forgive me. Because I have forgiveness in my own life, it is possible for me to forgive others.' [2]

North Korea has become synonymous with Communist brutality heaping unimaginable sufferings on the Christians of that isolated nation. Kim Il-sung created the state as we know it today. His mother was a genuine converted Christian woman, but he rejected her God and began the oppression against the church. Now the whole country is facing famine and starvation. During the Korean War (1950–53), 500 Christian missionaries were captured by the Communists and shot.

On 27 July 2009, Nigerian pastor George Orjih, along with other Christians, was beheaded by Islamist militants because of his love for Christ. Moments before his death he sent a message to his church: 'Tell my brothers that I died well and am living with Christ. And if we all die, we know that we die for the Lord.' Some of his companions survived and were able to take his final

'TELL MY BROTHERS THAT I DIED WELL AND AM LIVING WITH CHRIST'

'sermon' to his congregation.

Stories like these could fill volumes of books, but the question is, why should there be such antagonism to Jesus and His followers? There is growing hostility towards Christians in the West, but why?

Jesus repeatedly warned His followers that this would happen: 'Remember the word that I said to you, "A servant is not greater than his master. If they persecuted Me, they will also persecute you."'[3] It was the pattern of the early Christian church; the apostle Paul describes himself as 'persecuted, but not forsaken'[4] and writes about his many persecutions. Love is the essence of martyrdom, and in dying for Christ many Christians have seen themselves as imitators of Him.

'A SERVANT IS NOT GREATER THAN HIS MASTER'

Nobody, though, wishes persecution on themselves. It comes because of the deep-seated hatred from some people towards God their Maker. Sin is, in essence, defiance against God and His commands. Defiant disobedience towards God can rapidly spiral down to hatred towards Him. Sometimes, too, the vitriol is so irrational that Christians suspect that there is a greater power at work than mere human wickedness. Certainly the Bible teaches that there is a devil, Satan – a fallen angel with power that is limited – but who controls demonic forces and bears a bitter hatred towards God.

Jesus said of Satan that he loves to kill, steal and destroy. [5] There are outbursts of evil in the history of the world that appear inexplicable apart from being the work of Satan. One day, Satan, who has already been cast from God's presence, will be cast away from a position of power and influence in the world for ever. Until then, there will always be persecution of those who trust God and want to honour Him in all things. It is testimony to the truth of Jesus' warning words.

NOTES

1. John 1:29.

2. http://www.lifepositive.com/mind/ethics-and-values/forgiveness/gladys-staines.asp, accessed 20 May 2013.

3. John 15:20, NKJV.

4. 2 Corinthians 4:9, NKJV.

5. See John 10:10.

31

Have you ever wished you had the faith of your Christian friends?

Many times I have been told by sincere people that they wish they had my faith. I want to reply with words to the effect that it is not my faith they need, but my Jesus. Faith is not some mysterious ingredient owned by some but not others; nor is it a gene, rather like a congenital condition, which either you are born with or you are not. Faith is resting on what God has said, and any of us may do that.

We may display faith many times a day. We have faith, of a sort, when we get on a train that it will take us to our destination, when we sit on a chair believing it will support us, or when we go out for a meal assuming that it will be free of disease. These are simple examples of faith which we can readily have, both of past experience and because nothing supernatural is involved.

Faith in God is on a different level. Because God is spirit, for many that requires a greater step of faith. When God sent His Son, Jesus, into the world, He came from His spiritual realm in heaven to our earth. He 'bridged the gap', so that in 'seeing Him' we are 'seeing God'. Faith is simply taking the attitude that God has said what He has, and I am going to put my confidence in what He has said.

If you have genuine Christian friends, grill them and ask questions. Ask them to share what God means to them, how He has answered their specific prayers, and how you can come to a similar faith in Jesus.

Faith, which is a gift from God, comes through hearing the word of God. Therefore, I would encourage you to read the Bible for yourself. Start with the Gospels, Matthew, Mark, Luke and John in the New Testament, and let Jesus walk off the pages of the Bible and reveal Himself to you. Go to a church which believes and lives out traditional Christian beliefs and is passionate about explaining the gospel to their community. As you hear the Bible preached, you will find that faith grows.

FAITH, WHICH IS A GIFT FROM GOD, COMES THROUGH HEARING THE WORD OF GOD

32

What would stop you from putting your trust in Jesus Christ?

The West's preferred religion today appears to be secularism, with a distant nodding respect for God. Belief in God is viewed with superstition. It is regarded like the notion of touching wood – a safety net in case God is a reality and perhaps we will meet Him after death as the Judge of our eternal destiny.

However, the issues at stake are too great to be given a wide berth. Dramatically, the Old Testament prophet Ezekiel despaired of the casual way the Israelites were treating God and His commandments in view of the coming judgement. He said, 'A sword, a sword is sharpened... to make a sore slaughter... should we then make mirth?' [1] If it is at all true that there could be a God, and that He has demonstrated His love towards us by sending Jesus into the world to die for us, it *has* to be important.

If it is evidence you need, please look again at the

chapters where we examine the historical facts for the resurrection and the fulfilled prophecies of the Bible. Christians contend that God has revealed Himself through Jesus, so the evidence for His greatest miracle of raising Jesus back to life after His death is crucial. As well, He has revealed Himself through the Bible. One part of the evidence for its reliability is the fulfilment of prophecies. There are so many specific prophecies which centuries later proved to be true. Clearly, only God can see the future and reveal in the present, in tiny detail, what will happen, demonstrating that the prophets were inspired by God.

Perhaps you have been put off the church by someone who was acting hypocritically. Real Christians, however, are always ready to admit that they have acted wrongly – after all, it is the first step to coming to faith, to confess to God that we are guilty of sin – so there should be an admitting that mistakes were made. Once a person has become a Christian they will not want to deliberately act sinfully, though until heaven, we are never the people we want to be. Gradually, God works within believers to make them more and more like Jesus.

GOD WORKS WITHIN BELIEVERS TO MAKE THEM MORE AND MORE LIKE JESUS

On the other hand, it could be that what happened is evidence that the person is not really following Jesus. When Jesus was crucified He was stripped of His clothes, which were gambled for and presumably worn by the winner. In a similar way, ever since then many people have 'worn' the name 'Christian', even though it does not belong to them. Christians, though, are simply forgiven sinners, but the trait to sin continues with us, until we are changed and made like Jesus.

God never promises that we will have tomorrow. The Bible teaches that the time to get right with God is today. God may be speaking to you today, but He may not do so again. As well, if it really is true that Jesus loved us and gave Himself for us on the cross, why add another twenty-four hours of rejecting or neglecting Him as Lord, when you could start the joyful journey of living with Jesus right now?

Billy Sunday was a maverick preacher of the 1930s in the USA. He had been the top baseball player before his conversion to Christ. He defined an excuse as 'the skin of a reason blown up by lies, liable to go pop upon the pin prick of truth.' Excuses, in light of what God has done for us, appear lame and insulting – hardly the right response to almighty God.

NOTE

1. Ezekiel 21:9,10, KJV.

33

Do you sometimes wish you knew what or how to pray?

God, who brought all things into being, delights to hear us pray. Prayer is not superstition, like crossing our fingers and hoping for the best. It is not deluding ourselves with false hopes, like reading horoscopes. Neither is it vainly repeating set words. Rather, it is speaking to God, who is Lord of all.

Jesus encouraged us to pray, and promises that God will answer the prayers of His children when they pray according to His plans and purposes.

Prayer for us is very easy – we simply talk to God. It is so straightforward for us, but it was costly for God. He paid the greatest price of all so that we can pray to Him anytime, anywhere and about anything.

When Jesus was crucified, He actually took on Himself all the wrong of which we are guilty, so that if we believe on Him, we can be forgiven and come to know God. Once we have trusted the risen, living Jesus as our Lord, Saviour and Friend, it is natural to pray, to talk with Him. God is always ready to listen.

I have written some prayers you may find helpful to pray and personalise for your own situation.

A prayer of thanksgiving and praise

Dear God,

I worship You that You are God, and that there is no one else like You.

I praise You, heavenly Father, for the wonder of all creation; the sun, moon and stars, as well as the sparkling life around us. Thank You for life, and the purposes you have even for me.

I worship You, Lord Jesus, that even though I have sinned in thought, word and deed, you love me. I bless You that You came to earth as a baby and were willing to go to the cross and die for my sin. Thank You that You rose from the dead and are alive today.

Thank You, God, for the Holy Spirit, who is at work in our world today, pointing people to all that You have done. Thank You that He lives in all who receive Your mercy and forgiveness.

For all You have done for me, and mean to me, I praise and worship, counting my blessings and rejoicing in Your goodness. Amen.

A prayer for all times

Dear all-knowing God,

Thank You that You are God. Thank You that You are all-powerful, that You know all things, that You are everywhere and never change. I worship You, the one God: Father, Son and Holy Spirit.

Thank You for the life You have given me. You are God, and Lord over all. I am so thankful for who You are and all You have done. I take comfort from the Bible's teaching that one day every knee will bow before You and acknowledge Your rule and goodness.

I praise You that You, the Father, sent Jesus the Son to be the Saviour of the world. Help me to be truly sorry for all that is wrong in my life. I am so grateful that Jesus carried my sins in His own body on the cross. It is wonderful to me that Jesus paid the penalty for my sin, for I know that I do not deserve to be with You eternally, but Jesus has made a way back to You by His sacrifice on the cross. Thank You that Jesus rose again and is alive today as the loving Saviour and Friend of sinners.

I am grateful that the Holy Spirit is working in the world today. Thank You that He helps men, women and children believe and trust in Jesus as Lord and Saviour.

I pray for those I know and love, and ask that You

would be with them to protect and strengthen them in all that they do, wherever they will be today.

Help me to do the things that I should. May I know peace and joy, Your companionship and guidance moment by moment. Make me someone who always wants to help others without meddling in their affairs. And those in particular need, please draw near to them at this time.

I pray these prayers in the name of Jesus. Amen.

A morning prayer

Dear God,

Thank You for a safe night's sleep and now a new day. I need Your help as I face all that the day has in store for me. May I experience Your grace, guidance and gladness, Your strength and companionship, Your help in everything I do and say. I praise You that nothing that happens today will surprise You, for You know all things. Help me to cast all my cares upon You, for I know that You care for me.

Help me in all I do to show kindness and love to those around, and honour You in the things I say and do. I pray in the name of Jesus.

Amen.

An evening prayer

Dear God and Saviour,

Thank You for this past day, and the life You have given me to enjoy. Thank You for those I have met, for friends and family. Thank You for the food, drink and activities I have enjoyed. Thank You for all who have shown care for me and helped me in so many ways. Thank You for the beauty of the world around, and the wonder of creation. Thank You, too, that this life is not all there is. Thank You that there is eternity to be lived with You. Thank You for the place where there are no tears, no death, no mourning or crying, nor pain, for the former things have passed away.

Please forgive all the sins of this past day. I praise You that Jesus has paid the price for all that is unworthy of You in my life. Cleanse me from all that is wrong, and help me to live as I should, loving You and loving others.

I pray for a good night's sleep. Please watch over me, and keep me safe.

In Jesus' name, Amen.

A prayer for your nation

Dear heavenly King and Lord of all,

I thank You for my country, its heritage and culture, its beauty and diversity. I pray for those who are in authority both nationally and locally, that they would worship and obey You, and that they would govern with honesty and integrity. I pray that there would be godliness and righteousness in our land, and that all would be able to live quiet and peaceable lives. I pray that injustice and violence, impurity and all that is false would be done away with.

I pray this in the name of Jesus. Amen.

A prayer for your family

Dear heavenly Father,

I bless You for families, and for those whom I love and have known.

I pray for the elderly in my family circle [you may like to name them], that in their old age You would help them today. Keep them from cynicism, and grumbling, from loneliness and frustration, but help them to trust in You and find strength in You.

I pray for the children [again, name as many as you know and love]. Thank You for their joy and energy, their willingness to learn and ability to cheer. Keep them from evil: evil people, evil circumstances and evil influences. Help them today, and to grow to trust, love and serve You with selflessness and joy.

I pray for those close to me [naming them]. May they know the peace that comes from knowing You, and living the life You want them to live.

Unite my family that we might know joy and harmony, experiencing Your help day by day.

Hear these prayers, which I pray because of Jesus. Amen.

34

Would you be willing now to ask Jesus to become your Lord and Saviour and, with His help, start to follow Him?

God's love for you is so great, His willingness to bring you into a relationship with Himself has gone to such lengths, His patience with you is so enduring, His ability to forgive you and make all things new so powerful, your need of Him so absolute, and His invitation for you to join His family so powerfully demonstrated, that I would encourage and urge you to turn from all that keeps you from Him and ask Jesus to become your Lord and Saviour. A person gets married as they speak words of commitment to their would-be spouse. Similarly, becoming a Christian happens when you take words to God, but these are words of repentance and faith, trust and commitment to Him. You could pray with words like this:

O God, thank You that You know everything there is to know about me. I want to say that I am sorry for all my sin. With Your help I want to turn from it. Thank You for Your love towards me. Thank You that Jesus came into the world to live and then die, paying the penalty for all my wrongdoing. Thank You that He rose again from the dead. Please forgive me. By Your Holy Spirit, come to live in my life. Please become my Lord and Saviour... forever. Help me to follow Jesus and become more like Him. Thank You for hearing this prayer, which I pray in the name of Jesus. Amen.

If you have genuinely prayed this, God will have heard and will answer. God in His Word has promised that. Take time to start to cultivate your relationship with God, and begin to enjoy the wonderful new adventure of walking through life with God. I recommend the daily, dogged, delightful discipline of meeting with God for a time of reading the Bible and prayer. Reading the Bible book by book (maybe starting with the Gospels) allows God to teach and speak to you; as you pray, you in turn speak with Him. As you get involved in a Bible-believing church (sadly, not all of them are), you will be able to worship and serve the Lord in the community and security of God's people. Church is a great family in which to grow strong in the Christian faith.

Genuine Christians don't confine themselves to the church family. They want to serve others, and to let them see and hear how Jesus has changed them. I love the privilege, and you will too, of sharing with others the good news of the gospel: that God has loved us, despite our rebellion against Him, and sent His Son to suffer, die and rise again so that we might know Him throughout life, through death and then into eternity. Christians love Jesus because He first loved us and gave Himself for us on the cross; now we love telling others about Him.

For more information, please look at www.tell-me-more.org

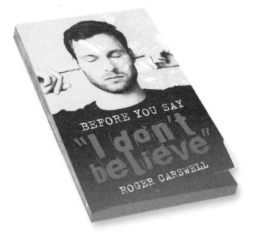

10Publishing is the publishing house of **10ofThose**.
It is committed to producing quality Christian
resources that are biblical and accessible.

www.10ofthose.com is our online retail arm selling
thousands of quality books at discounted prices.
We also service many church bookstalls
and can help your church to set up a bookstall.
Single and bulk purchases welcome.

For information contact: **sales@10ofthose.com**
or check out our website: **www.10ofthose.com**